UNDERSTANDING TOMORROW

Lyle E. Schaller

ABINGDON
Nashville

UNDERSTANDING TOMORROW

Copyright © 1976 by Abingdon

Library of Congress Cataloging in Publication Data

Schaller, Lyle E. Understanding tomorrow.
1. United States—Social conditions—1960.
2. Social change. 3. Forecasting. I. Title.
HN65.S412   309.1'73'0925   75-38693

ISBN 0-687-42978-1

MANUFACTURED   BY   THE   PARTHENON   PRESS   AT
NASHVILLE, TENNESSEE, UNITED STATES OF AMERICA

Contents

Introduction

"By 1975, there will be little inflation and plenty of jobs." "An unmanned satellite aircraft will have flown to outer space beyond 200 miles out." "The cars of 1975 will bear little resemblance to those of today." "A telephone in nearly every room of the average home will be considered essential." These four are among the predictions made in 1955 by a group of national leaders about what 1975 would bring. They had been sealed in a time capsule at the Prudential Insurance Company's main office in Minneapolis. The capsule was opened in June, 1975.

These four examples illustrate several helpful concepts in looking at the future.

First, it is very difficult to predict the future in specific terms. Writing in 1914 John and Evelyn Dewey listed the many technological complications facing the child of that day including railways, steamboats, and telephones, but did not mention the automobile.[1] Writing in 1958 about an affluent society John Kenneth Galbraith failed to include the black revolution as a major factor to be reckoned with in the 1960s.[2] In the late 1950s and early 1960s many highly respected scientists and science writers including Edward Teller, C. P. Snow, and Gerard Piel anticipated that the computer would radically alter society and produce an automatic world ruled by electronic machines. In 1962 President John F. Kennedy declared that adjusting to automation would be the greatest domestic challenge of the sixties. Many credited the computer with a form of "artificial intelligence." It now is clear that the computer is only a machine that can manipulate a very limited arena of data according to instructions. It cannot think and is not about to do all of man's routine work, much less rule society.[3]

As the year 1984 moves closer, the book with that title by George Orwell is less and less threatening— although in 1974 many people wrote about "seven years from now" or "a dozen years hence" rather than use the convenient time frame of a decade, which returned to popularity in 1975. Presumably in 1979 planning and projections will be in multiples of three years rather than five years for that one twelve-month period.

It is very difficult, and usually impossible, to predict the future in detail. The temptations to simply project existing customs, traditions, habits, and ways of doing things are overwhelming.

A second concept that is useful in seeking to understand tomorrow is that while technological changes may occur very rapidly, they are difficult to predict. To at least one leader in 1955 a spacecraft that could travel 200 miles from earth would be a tremendous step for man to take in twenty years. To Neil Armstrong, only fourteen years later, "That's one small step for a man, one giant leap for mankind."

Between 1600 and 1650 prices in England tripled, but the price of firewood increased eight times. As wood became increasingly scarce the English government responded in a predictable manner by urging conservation measures. In 1593 beer exporters were required to return the original beer barrels to England or import sufficient lumber of the appropriate quality to make replacement barrels. What was not predictable was that this energy shortage would lead to the use of coal as a replacement for wood in heating and manufacturing, the development of the steam engine, the development first of a canal system and later of railroads, and eventually the Industrial Revolution.[4] Now in the last half of the 1970s the shortage of firewood is a major issue in many Third World nations.

Today many people discuss the "energy shortage." A more precise statement would be to describe a shortage of low-priced petroleum. The world is filled with abundant sources of energy, most of which are yet to be harnessed. A reasonable prediction about the future is that sometime before the end of this century, and probably long before 1990, there will be (a) a technological breakthrough to replace petroleum as a basic source of fuel with a cleaner and more powerful source and (b) a sharp drop in the world market price of petroleum. Which of these will happen first is unpredictable, but very important!

A third useful concept to remember in understanding tomorrow is that while technological changes often occur at a comparatively rapid pace, such as the advances in the exploration of space, changes affecting interpersonal relationships usually occur at a comparatively slow pace (see chap. 18). People are able and willing to adapt to technological changes much more rapidly than to changes affecting social patterns and interpersonal relationships. That is one reason why the nuclear family and the worshiping congregation have survived every change for centuries.

A fourth useful concept for looking at the future also is illustrated by the Prudential time capsule. While the passage of time brings changes, the changes usually are in the direction of increasing the complexity of life, not in decreasing it. Nevertheless, most predictions about the future include the expectation that the future will bring less complexity. In fact, while the nature of the complexity of life changes, life tends to become more and more complicated for the average person (see chap. 13). This suggests that the reader should beware of any proposed change which promises to make life simpler!

In looking at the future and in reading this volume it may be helpful to look at a few of the many different approaches used by futurists.

Perhaps the most common approach is reflected by the contents of the Prudential time capsule. This is the simple prediction about the future such as the one submitted by Dr. Charles Mayo in 1955 when he predicted that by 1975 "a way of avoiding many forms of the common cold may be found" or the one submitted by another contributor: "Railroads will enjoy substantial passenger business."

A second approach to the future is the scenario popularized by Herman Kahn and Anthony J. Wiener. The scenario is an attempt to describe in some detail an imaginative simulation of a situation set several years in the future and to document this with the hypothetical sequence of events leading to that situation.[5]

A more frequently used approach is the projection of trends into the future. This approach was used by this writer in an earlier volume which included the probable consequences of twenty different trends.[6]

A fourth approach is to pick one year as a watershed year and suggest how the future will be influenced by the events of that year. One example of this would be the use of 1950 as a dividing year (see chap. 3) marking the shift from survival goals to an emphasis on role and identity. Another example would be to pick 1967 as such a watershed year. Among the many diverse but distinctive characteristics of that year, 1967 marked the escalation of the Vietnam conflict to that irreversible point that divided the nation; the open recognition of the identity crisis in American society, the institutionalization of the longest inflationary era in America's economic history; the "victory" of campus ministers over the senior pastors of near-campus congregations in the struggle for recognition as the focal point for ministry to students; the recognition of futurism as an important academic discipline, the shift from racial equality to the more inclusive focus of the Big Revolution (see chap. 1); the beginnings of the disengagement by Christian churches in the United States from their relationships with the Christian churches on other continents; the flowering of the New Towns Movement (which wilted again in the mid-1970s); the leveling off and the beginning of a continuing decline in the number of people institutionalized in prisons, mental hospitals, homes for unwed mothers, and institutions for emotionally disturbed children; the beginnings of major deficits in institutions of higher education; the beginning of the reversal of the rural-to-urban migration that began one hundred and fifty years earlier and had been interrupted only by the Great Depression of the 1930s (see chap. 9); and the shift to independent off-campus living by tens of thousands of university and college students. Yes, 1967 was the year that was! It was a watershed year and offers one approach for looking at the future.

A fifth approach that is gaining increasing use is the

"alternative futures" concept which provides a broader base than the scenario for evaluating alternative courses of action. A simple example of this is that used by the Bureau of Census in making population projections. Traditionally they offered Series A, B, C, and D with the basic variable being the number of children a woman would bear during her lifetime. As births, or more precisely the fertility rate, continued to drop the Series A was replaced by a Series E, and in 1972 the Series B was replaced by a Series F. The alternative futures forecast by the Bureau of the Census reflected the decline in births (see chap. 7).

A sixth approach is used by the "gloom and doom" school of futurists and extends from the Old Testament prophets through the Reverend Thomas Malthus, who predicted in 1798 that the increase in population always would outrun any increases in food supply and thus the masses always would be on the verge of starvation, to the Club of Rome.[7] An extreme form of this approach to the future leads one to look to that day when all of the residents of the United States are crowded into Arizona, New Mexico, and Texas while the rest of the nation is covered by filing cabinets and cemeteries!

A seventh approach is to think in terms of cycles or stages and to project into the future from this frame of reference. A simple example is the sixty-eight-year-old person who is dying and uses Elisabeth Kübler-Ross's five stages of looking at death—denial, anger, bargaining, depression, and acceptance—to look into what the future may hold.[8] Another example is the three stages that technological advances usually follow—first, as a replacement for previous technology; second, the perception by innovative and creative people of the potential in the new technological advance; and third, the mass application of the technological development. This concept can be illustrated with the steam engine, the automobile, the airplane, television, computers, digital watches, and nuclear power.

Occasionally the application of this concept becomes far more subjective and complex. An example of this would be the various cycles used by economists which include the forty-month Kitchin cycle, the nine- to ten-year Juglar cycle, and the fifty-year Kondratieff cycle. (Incidentally, application of Kondratieff cycle suggests an economic downturn from 1971 into the early 1990s.) While the Joseph Schumpeter school of cyclical theory in economics has been losing out to the W. W. Rostow proponents of the theory of self-sustaining and self-generating economic growth in recent years, it offers an interesting example of the use of this concept of looking into the future.

An eighth approach to the future constitutes the basic frame of reference for this volume. This is to offer a series of generalizations which attempt to identify the central issue in broader terms and to explain what is happening. This might be described as "putting the generalization over the specific." What is a useful generalization for understanding the gap between the leaders of a group and the members of that group? "What is true for the individual will not necessarily be true for the society or organization as a whole" is one attempt to explain not only the leader-group gap, but also parent-child relationships, conflicts between religious denominational agencies and congregations, differences between teachers and students, and disagreements between publishers and authors. This is a very simple and useful generalization which the Big Revolution has made increasingly relevant, but it continues to be neglected.

Another example of this approach to the future is that as a society becomes more complex (see chap. 13), social selection evolves from a hereditary class structure to a response to merit to a dependence on credentials to (let the reader fill in the next stage in this generalization).

This volume consists of an attempt to offer twenty-one such generalizations for understanding tomorrow and to suggest some of the implications and consequences of these generalizations. The first nine chapters discuss major substantial changes in American society. The next eight chapters describe eight changes which are both the products and the causes of other changes while the final chapter offers four generalizations to help the reader live more comfortably with tomorrow as it arrives. It should be fun!

The origins of this book go back many years to the author's earlier career as a city planner and the related interests in futurism and change. Out of these and subsequent experiences emerged the conviction that often it is helpful to look at the larger picture, to see details and specific incidents from the context of a larger perspective, to look beyond symptoms to problems and to survey the forest in addition to examining the individual trees. The eighteen chapters in this volume represent an attempt to bring together a series of generalizations which will help the reader understand the world of today as well as the world of tomorrow more adequately.

While it is impossible for anyone to identify all of the biases and prejudices the writer brings to a volume such as this, there are four which may help the reader in identifying the author's perspective. First, I believe God is at work in his world. Second, this is written from an optimistic rather than a pessimistic view of what tomorrow will bring. Third, much of what we know is not true and much of what we try will not work, but frequently as we fail to "solve" problems, we do succeed in "trading up" and have a better, more enjoyable, and more challenging batch of new problems to work with after we trade—even though we thought we were solving, not trading problems. Fourth, the increasing complexity of life does represent a more sensitive concern for people, and that is good!

Finally, I am grateful to the many people who have shared their wisdom and insights with me through what they have said and what they have written. While they are far too numerous to name here, I am in their debt and I acknowledge it!

To Agnes

1
The Big Revolution

What do the following have in common?

In November, 1974, seventy-five new Democratic congressmen were sent to Washington by the voters. The traditional advice to new members of the House of Representatives has been "To get along, go along." These freshmen congressmen were influential in unseating three committee chairmen and in sharply curtailing the reliance on seniority in selecting House leaders.

Among the landmark verdicts of the Supreme Court during the second half of this century have been the decisions which outlawed racially segregated schools, required state legislatures to be reapportioned on a "one man, one vote" basis after every decennial census, and prohibited religious exercises in public schools.

For 60 years the Boy Scouts' manual, *Handbook for Boys,* remained almost unchanged and 26 million copies were printed. In 1972 a completely new manual, the *Scout Handbook,* was issued. Among other changes were inclusion of a chapter on drug abuse, a section on rat bites, a unit on combating water and air pollution, and many pictures which showed black boys engaged in scouting activities. Among the items omitted from the new manual were the traditional sections on wigwagging, map making, and edible plants.

In the depression year of 1935, 20 million men's suits were sold. Thirty-five years later, despite the increase in the adult male population and the huge increase in expenditures for men's clothing, only 16 million men's suits were sold in the United States.

In 1945 it was very difficult for a woman to gain admittance to medical school. Few classes had more than one or two women. By 1975, 18 percent of the students in medical schools are women and it is expected that by 1985 this figure will have increased to 30 percent.

Instead of building automobiles on an assembly line, Volvo employs persons to work together as a team in putting an automobile together.

In state after state the courts have declared that the schools do not have the authority to determine the length of a boy's hair, to prohibit beards and mustaches, or to impose a rigid dress code on the students.

In a growing number of Protestant churches the traditional nominating committee has been replaced by a process which encourages self-nomination and the members nominate themselves for the leadership position they would like to hold.[1]

In early 1975 the state-operated Kansas Industries for the Blind paid blind workers $1.63 an hour to stuff mattresses while paying sighted workers $2.10 an hour for the same work. After a two-week protest by blind workers the organization agreed to change the compensation schedule.

In one of the most important religious liberty decisions of this century, the United States Supreme Court ruled **7 to 0 on May 15, 1972, that the Wisconsin state law** requiring Amish children to attend high school violated the free exercise of religion clause of the First Amendment of the Constitution. The Court pointed out that "modern compulsory secondary education in rural areas is now largely carried on in a consolidated school, often remote from the student's home and alien to his daily home life." In its ruling the Court noted that "the values and programs of the modern secondary school are in sharp conflict with the fundamental mode of life mandated by the Amish religion."

All ten of these illustrations carry a common theme. Each one is an example of a basic concept in understanding tomorrow. Each one illustrates one dimension of the Big Revolution. Each one represents an example of the expansion of the rights of the individual and a reduction of the pressures of the culture on the individual.

The Big Revolution of modern history began in the first years after World War II and is still in progress. For centuries people were trained to fit into the existing structures, patterns, schedules, and traditions of the culture. The Big Revolution is changing that. Increasingly the emphasis is to change the culture to accommodate people and to affirm the differences among people. Under the umbrella of this larger change can be placed such movements as black liberation, women's liberation, youth liberation, gay liberation, and scores of other pressures for changing the patterns of society.

This trend will be of greater assistance in helping the reader understand the changes being brought about by our movement into the future than any other concept in this volume. The person who can grasp the nature and the direction of the Big Revolution will have an enormous advantage over those who do not comprehend this concept in both understanding and in responding to the changes that are a part of the second half of the twentieth century.

Closely related to the concept described by the Big Revolution is a basic principle of planned change. Normally, rejection is the initial response to any new idea that involves changing existing structures, customs, or schedules. This does *not* automatically mean *final* rejection. All it means is that the normal reaction to any new idea is to reject it. It may or may not be adopted when it is reintroduced later. Frequently proposals for change are rejected two or three or four times before they are accepted. Many happily married readers can recall that the first proposal for a change in their marital status from single to married was rejected when suggested. Most of the proposals to consolidate rural school districts to create a larger financial base and a larger student body were rejected when first proposed but the number of school districts in the United States dropped from 108,579 in 1942 to 50,446 in 1957 to 15,781 in 1972.

The person who can put together these two concepts of the Big Revolution and the normal response to this initial introduction of a proposal for change not only will have a far above average ability to *understand* what tomorrow will bring, but often will be able to *predict* what tomorrow will bring!

What Are the Consequences?

The consequences of the Big Revolution are all about us. They can be seen in the rapid strides taken by blacks, women, and youth after centuries of being kept in a second-class relationship by the structures, institutions, and traditions created by white adult males.

The consequences can be seen in hundreds of cities where the curbs by the sidewalk now have a sloping incline down to the street to accommodate people in wheelchairs. The consequences can be seen in an increasing number of ordinances and statutes that require all new public buildings to be designed to accommodate the handicapped.

The consequences can be seen in the struggle within the Episcopal Church over the ordination of women and in the categorical "Yes!" offered by Roman Catholic priest-psychologist Father Eugene Kennedy and priest-sociologist Father Andrew Greeley when each was asked, "Do you expect to see the Roman Catholic Church ordain women in your lifetime?" [2]

The consequences can be seen in the public schools, which while still managed primarily for the benefit of the administration and the teachers rather than the students, are beginning to repeal some rules and change others to accommodate the students.

The Big Revolution is at the heart of the power struggle in the Lutheran Church—Missouri Synod over whether the supreme administrative authority of the denomination rests in the congregations or in St. Louis.

The Big Revolution is behind the radical changes which have taken place within the Army when the military draft was not extended and the armed forces had to depend on volunteers. "We had to turn the Army around to meet the volunteers, not vice versa," was the way Major General William B. Fulton summarized the changes when he was commanding general at Fort Lewis.

The Big Revolution is what has changed LeCorbusier (the professional name of the Swiss architect Charles Edouard Jeanneret) from a hero for "establishment architects" to an irrelevant figure out of the past for those architects who recognize that buildings should be designed for the interaction and socializing of people rather than for cover stories in architectural journals or for picture postcards. The new "humane architecture" is a product of the Big Revolution and is supportive, not disruptive of the social interaction of people.

The Big Revolution is the basic force behind the efforts to humanize work and to encourage job fulfillment.

The Big Revolution is the basic reason why it is unusual to see a Protestant minister in a white shirt or a Methodist woman wearing a hat to church. Among the many other consequences of the Big Revolution are the increase in the divorce rate, the decrease in the proportion of high school graduates going to college, the exodus of thousands of priests from the ranks of the active clergy in the Roman Catholic Church, and the rapid increase in the number of female executives in large corporations.

Perhaps the most neglected but far-reaching implication of the Big Revolution is that it will continue to create a very serious imbalance in the composition of the population. This concept of a population imbalance can be illustrated very easily. All across the nation there are thousands of persons holding a position which includes in the job title the word "coordinator." The number of persons holding the position of coordinator probably exceeds by a 1,000 to 1 margin the number of people in the labor force who feel their greatest need is to have someone coordinate them and/or their work!

Similarly the Big Revolution is producing another imbalance in the composition of the population. The number of persons who want to tell others what they can or cannot do continues to grow, while the number who are looking for someone to tell them what they can or cannot do is shrinking very rapidly. (Most of the opponents of a "permissive society" are to be found in that growing first category of the population.)

A second seriously neglected, but far more complex implication of the Big Revolution concerns the way organizations and institutions in American society are structured for decision-making. In accord with the Puritan tradition and the concept of majority rule, most organizations and institutions are structured in a manner to tell people what they cannot do. This has turned out to be an exceptionally effective method of smothering creativity and discouraging initiative. The larger, the more complex, and the more top heavy with senior administrators, the more likely the organization will be structured to tell people what they cannot do.

A simple but very clear example of the impact of the Big Revolution on persons in positions of authority who had yielded to the temptation to tell people what they cannot do can be illustrated by three actions of the Board of Trustees of a church-owned and operated home for the elderly in Topeka, Kansas. In 1953 the Board declared that a romance between a resident and an employee of the home was sufficient cause for dismissal of the employee. A year later the Board declared that if two residents of the home married after admission they must find a home elsewhere. By 1956, however, the impact of the Big Revolution was being felt in Topeka in many, many different ways and when an elderly couple married they were permitted to remain in the home.

This tendency of organizations to tell people what they cannot do has become an acute problem in government and in nonprofit voluntary associations. The comparatively low productivity of many governmental departments is one result of this. The growing resistance to zoning laws and land use regulations which determine who can live in middle and upper class residential neighborhoods represents a clash between the traditional approach to decision-making and The Big Revolution. The discussions in the 1970s over the decriminalization of victimless crimes and the repeal of many laws, statutes, and ordinances governing personal behavior patterns represents the impact of the Big Revolution on the Puritan conscience. The rebellion of the 1970s against big government is another consequence of the Big Revolution and the concern that government function as an enabling force rather than as a restrictive agent.

One of the more creative responses to this issue is appearing in many voluntary associations where the procedures are being changed to count the "yes" votes rather than the "no" votes. In very simple terms this means that on programmatic proposals no attempt is made to cause the opposition to be counted. Instead program is developed in a manner that asks, "Are there enough resources (people, time, money, energy, expertise, etc.) available that can be mobilized to implement this proposal?" If the answer is in the affirmative, that is a decision to approve proceeding with implementation of the proposal. The votes of those who would be opposed to the proposal are not counted. Since those "no" votes will not be counted, there is no reason to cause people to line up in opposition.[3]

For much of the life of the United States as a nation, the basic alternative to the pressures on the individual to conform to the "civilized" East was to follow the frontier westward. Eventually, however, the frontier disappeared and a subsequent response to the closing of the frontier was the Big Revolution. Another response was a significant change in the dynamics of how the older generation "civilizes" the next generation. This change also is an important element in understanding tomorrow.

2
Who Civilized Whom?

For centuries a basic function of every culture and society has been to "civilize" the children and youth to fit into that culture. When used in a technical sense, "civilize" means to educate or bring out of a rude state into a more refined state. The parents and the entire tribe or group or society usually share a responsibility for carrying out this civilizing function. Various elements of this civilizing process are illustrated by the North American Indian tribes teaching the young boys to be hunters and warriors; by the college fraternity of the 1920s which taught new members to conform; by basic training in the Marine Corps; by the all-day preparation for the church dinner in which the new bride from another county and another religious denomination, recently married to a local lad, was initiated into that church tribe in the 1930s; by the IBM on-the-job training program for a young college graduate; and by the rookie policeman riding in a patrol car with a veteran police officer.

Regardless of the culture, age, and local circumstances there have always been two constant factors in the civilizing process. First, the older people train the younger members of the society in the folkways of that culture. Second, those doing the civilizing normally greatly outnumber those being civilized. It is a rare and memorable era when either one of these conditions is reversed. One example of this happened in A.D. 410 when the Visigoths captured and sacked Rome. Another is when white Europeans "civilized" the American Indians. Usually, however, the civilizing process proceeds very quietly and the older majority instructs the much smaller and younger minority in the customs and traditions of that culture.

It may be helpful for the person seeking to understand tomorrow to review the most recent occasion in the United States when the civilizing forces were at least partially overwhelmed by those being civilized. When this happened it produced a minor revolution with long lasting effects.

The time period for the civilizing of young people in the United States gradually has been lengthened through a combination of many factors including demands for more formal education before a person enters the labor force and informal pressures to restrict the number of persons entering the labor force in any one year. For many years the civilizing period for young Americans has been from approximately age fourteen to age twenty-four.

In 1890 there were 14 million residents of the United States in the 14–24 age bracket. This number increased rather rapidly to 16.5 million in 1900 and to 20 million in 1910 (partly as a result of the great wave of immigration described in chap. 8) and then increased very slowly to 21.2 million in 1920 and to 24.9 million in 1930. Between 1929 and 1959 the number of persons in this age group fluctuated between a low of 24.2 million in 1952 and a high of 26.5 in 1941.

In very simple terms, for thirty years this nation had the task of instructing a group, which included approximately 25 million young persons at any one time, in the customs and traditions of American society. The number of people in this age group remained relatively constant for more than three decades. At the same time, however, the number of people responsible for doing the civilizing, those adults age twenty-five and over, jumped by nearly 60 percent from 62 million in 1929 to 98 million in 1959. The size of the job to be done remained approximately the same while the number of people responsible for doing that job increased by nearly 60 percent.

After a society or culture has informally prepared itself for the task of civilizing the young, this process tends to be sensitive to the changes in the ratio of the numbers of people in each group. Thus as the number of people in the over-twenty-four age group continued to increase at a relatively rapid pace and the number of persons in the 14–24 age bracket remained the same, there was a risk of "over-civilizing" the young. This may be a description of what happened to produce the "quiet generation" of young people of the 1950s. The civilizing forces greatly outnumbered those being civilized and the result was a generation of young people who followed rather docilely in the footsteps of their elders.

What happened in the 1960s?

First, the number of persons responsible for civilizing the young, those age twenty-five and over, increased from 92 million in 1959 to 99 million in 1969, an increase of approximately 9 percent.

The size of the job increased tremendously, however, as the number of young persons age 14–24 rose from 26.3 in 1959 (all figures exclude Alaska and Hawaii for the sake of comparability) to nearly 39 million in 1969.

When 1960 arrived the civilizing forces outnumbered the young by a 7 to 2 margin, but by the end of that decade that margin had shrunk to a 5 to 2 ratio.

What is more significant is that the society had geared up in the 1930s, 1940s, and 1950s for the task of civilizing a group of young persons which consisted of approximately 25 million. After thirty years of functioning with that work load spread over an ever increasing number of older people, its size was altered radically in the 1960s. Instead of a growing number of older people civilizing the same number of younger people, a pattern which had prevailed for as long as most older adults could remember, the number of people to be instructed in the customs and traditions of the culture increased by a greater number of persons than it had grown by in the previous seventy years!

What made the task even more difficult than these figures suggest, however, were three other factors.

The first of these was the Big Revolution which called into serious question and ultimately resulted in the rejection of the basic foundation stone of the whole concept of the civilizing process. Why should younger people be willing to be instructed on how to fit into the existing structures, institutions, systems, customs, traditions, schedules, and patterns of the culture? This was a very disturbing question, especially when many older people discovered they could not come up with an answer that was satisfying either to themselves or to many of the young people. Why should a high school student keep his hair cut short? Why should every college or university student actively support the football team? Why should a minister always wear a white shirt? Why should kids stay off drugs when it is permissible for adults to get drunk on alcohol? Why should a young man automatically rally around his flag when the nation finds itself overcommitted to a conflict in Vietnam? Why should older people who start wars be able to draft young men to fight them? Why should every high school student plan on going to college if at all possible? Why should blacks be expected to act as second-class citizens? Why should every young woman "learn her place" and move into it as quickly as possible? Why should so many jobs be barred to blacks and women? Why should every Mexican-American be expected to be happy doing manual labor?

The second factor which made the civilizing task even more difficult in the 1960s was the shift from survival goals to questions of identity, a trend which is the central theme of the next chapter.

The third factor which helped upset the whole civilizing process in the 1960s was that to describe the shift in the proportion of people in the two groups as a change from a ratio of 7 to 2 in 1959 to 5 to 2 ten years later is deceptive. The change really was more like from 7 to 2 to 4 to 3. The reason was that many of the adults in the civilizing group left their allies to unite with the "young barbarians," the people who were supposed to be the object of the civilizing process.

What happened?

To a substantial degree the young people who were to be influenced and trained by their elders reversed the flow and instructed or civilized or converted the older generation to the value systems, perspectives, and expectations of the younger generation.

Also to a very substantial degree other older people failed to understand what was happening and why the young people were not accepting the civilizing influences of their elders. Many older people saw what was happening and deeply resented it. After all, they had accepted the teachings of their elders when they were young. Why should this generation of young people be able to evade that process? (The unhappiness expressed by some of them is reflected in the first several paragraphs of the next chapter.)

Before going on to identify three of the major consequences of these developments of the 1960s, it may be helpful to remind the reader that this issue was a major concern of many people only a few years ago. As late as June, 1970, a Gallup poll reported that a majority of Americans considered "campus unrest" to be "the nation's *main* problem." Some readers may find that hard to believe today!

Three Major Consequences

Perhaps the most highly visible consequence of these changes in the civilizing processes was to create the mirage of a "generation gap." If there is a generation gap it can be described more accurately in terms of social class or value systems or from the perspective of the next chapter than from what happened in the 1960s. What has so often been described as a generation gap is not a gap between generations as much as it is a difference between perspectives and value systems.

For the purposes of understanding tomorrow the first significant consequence of the rapid increase in the size of the 14–24 age group can be illustrated by looking at the high school and college students of the 1960s when so many Americans believed campus unrest to be the nation's number one problem.

The young people of the 1960s had questions to ask, values to express, and concerns to share. In many cases they concluded they were not being heard. What is the normal response of the man who believes no one is hearing what he is saying? The normal response is to increase the volume. In the 1960s many high school and college students did not believe they were heard by their elders. In an effort to be heard they used several different approaches to attract attention, one of which was to turn up the volume.

As Margaret Mead has suggested, these "the oldest postwar people" [1] grew up in a world in which they were in fact the first born. No one born before the early 1940s ever grew up in a world in which the solar system was being explored by men in spaceships, in which television had created a completely new means of communication and socialization, in which man had the power to destroy all human life on the planet, in which a train of thought was regularly interrupted by commercials, in which it was not uncommon to have close friends who had lived on another continent, in which battles were reported in living color in one's own living room the same day they were being fought, and in which the Big Revolution was a reality.

In Miss Mead's words, "When the senior citizens of [this] new generation looked with horror on what their elders had wrought, and [they] clamored, often with more vigor than wisdom, for their own role." [2]

Many of the people who were experiencing this postwar world in their formative years were on the college and university campuses in the 1960s. To a very significant degree, however, they were there alone. The teachers and administrators had been born into and had been civilized in a prewar world. They could not hear what was being said by people in the group they were being hired to civilize.

The second generation to be born into this postwar world, the babies born in the 1952–60 era went off to college in the 1970s found a completely different environment on the campus. They found hundreds of graduate students, instructors, assistant professors, and administrators from that earlier first postwar generation. When the students who were born in the 1950s asked questions or offered criticisms of the system they found people who could hear and understand what they were saying. Therefore they did not have to raise their voices or turn up the volume. Part of the civilizing responsibility was being passed on to the older members of this first postwar generation. One result was that it became relatively quiet on the campus in the 1970s.

A second and related consequence of the combination of this reversal of the civilizing process and of the Big Revolution is that American society will never be the same again. The voting age will not be raised back up to twenty-one. Blacks will not be transformed back into second-class citizens. Jobs and leadership roles which have been opened up to women will not be returned to a "males only" category. Alternative newspapers will continue to be published by high school students. Homosexuals will not go back into the closet. Pedagogical styles will not return to the fifty-minute lecture with no time for questions. People will continue to ask both "Why?" and "Why not?"

The civilizing process, which for centuries was directed at training the young to live in the world of their elders has become a two-way process in which people born after 1945 have to instruct those born before 1940 in how to live in a postwar world.

The third consequence carries us back to looking at

numbers again. As was pointed out earlier, the 14–24 age bracket, the group on which a society naturally tends to focus its civilizing efforts, was relatively stable in size from 1929 to 1954 with approximately 26 million people in that age group. During the 1960s the number of people of this age jumped to 39 million, a 50 percent increase after three decades of stability.

During the 1970s this age group will increase by only 13 percent to 44 million. During the 1980s the number of persons aged 14–24 *will drop by approximately 20 percent* to 35 million! By the year 2000 there will be perhaps 38 to 40 million people in this age bracket—although that is obviously speculation since the oldest of this age group in the year 2000 will be born in 1976 and the youngest in 1986.

These figures suggest that it is unlikely that anyone born before 1940—and probably anyone born before 1950—will ever live through a decade paralleling the 1960s when the age group to be civilized increased so rapidly in numbers that they reversed the process. That is an important factor in understanding tomorrow!

In order to understand tomorrow more adequately it also is necessary to look at a radical change in the value system of the culture which coincided with the Big Revolution and the reversal of the civilizing process. This is the shift from a primary emphasis on survival goals to a primary emphasis on identity and role.

3
From Survival To Identity

"What this country really needs is another Great Depression," exclaimed a man in his sixties with a closely cropped head of white hair as he and two of his friends were discussing the economic recession of 1973–76. "If this recession turns into a genuine depression it'll teach some of these young people what it's all about! They'll learn the importance of hard work, the value of a dollar, and why it's a good idea to lay a little money aside for a rainy day!"

"I hear what you're saying, Bill, but you're all wrong," replied his friend Ed Maloney in a soothing tone of voice. "You're out of date in your thinking. I must admit I think as you do most of the time, but that doesn't mean we're both right. All that means is that we both were brought up in the same era. We were both teen-agers during the Great Depression and we're still reflecting in our thinking what we learned then. I've always known deep in my gut," he continued, as he patted a very generous stomach, "that I would die by starvation and I suppose this may represent a subconscious attempt to postpone that day, but in my head I know I'm not going to die of starvation. I may die in a more painful way, but you and I both know I won't starve to death."

"Years ago I heard a minister say you can tell how old you are by how you view death," added George Wilson. "He said that when you're young you look at death and ask, 'If?' When you're middle-aged you ask, 'When?' When you're old, you ask, 'How?' It seems to me we're beginning to sound like three old men. You're just jealous of the young people, Bill, because they're young and we're all getting old."

"You fellows aren't hearing what I'm saying," insisted the first man. "My dad taught me how to work and the value of a dollar, but none of these kids today know how to work, they don't care to learn, and they expect the government or somebody else will take care of them in their old age. Instead of learning from their elders as we all did when we were young, they're trying to make us be like them. Look at you, Ed, besides being fat, you look like you haven't had a haircut in at least six months!"

"I do hear what you're saying, Bill," replied Ed Maloney somewhat impatiently, "and I can assure you that on many occasions I've thought the same thoughts you're expressing now. But I'm afraid the problem is with you and me, not with the kids of today. If you want to get a new perspective on this issue, go down to the library and read this book by William Glasser called *The Identity Society.*"

A very useful frame of reference for examining the content of this discussion is Glasser's book.[1]

Glasser's basic contention is that following the end of World War II our society entered a new era. Up until the middle of this century everyone knew the primary question was "How do I survive?" For generations Americans had been reared in a culture that emphasized survival goals. This attitude or value system, which may have appeared threatened by obsolescene in the 1920s, was reinforced by the Great Depression which affirmed that survival was still the number one question for most people. The importance of survival goals was affirmed by the Puritan work ethic, Ben Franklin, life on the frontier, the Republican Party, the Protestant churches, most commencement addresses, and the attack on Pearl Harbor on December 7, 1941. World War II reinforced this priority given to survival goals.

Thus for generations the entire civilizing process in American culture emphasized this priority on survival goals. Anyone born before the late 1940s was born into an era and subjected to a conditioning process which emphasized the primacy of survival goals.

According to Glasser this changed in the middle of this century and the title of his book suggests what he sees as the distinguishing characteristic of the new era.

Glasser writes that he discovered this concept by examining why some public school teachers were successful and some were not effective. He concluded that the ineffective teachers followed the traditional pattern of giving a child recognition only within the context of learning. By contrast the successful teachers involved themselves with the students in a manner that helped the children see they were important human beings and recognized as persons, not solely as students.

While this is both a simplification and an expansion of Glasser's theory, perhaps the easiest way to explain this concept is that for centuries mankind was engaged in a struggle to survive. About a quarter of a century ago this struggle was replaced as the number one agenda item by the quest for identity. Anyone born before 1945 grew up in a world that stressed survival and in a world filled with institutions that reinforced this concept. People went to school to get an education (a survival goal) rather than to discover themselves as persons. In this survival-oriented world the primary motivating factor was power.

During the past twenty-five years the agenda has been changed. More and more people are primarly concerned with a search for recognition as persons.

What Are the Implications?

In looking at tomorrow there are several very important implications in this shift from primacy of survival goals to the quest for identity.

First, it is becoming apparent that people are finding more meaning in their lives from recognition and acceptance as persons than from recognition as the performer of a task. This change is more apparent in younger people than in older persons, but it is spread all across society.

This concept helps explain why a person may resign from a high paying or prestigious job in order to move into a vocation which helps the quest for identity.

This concept helps explain the rising divorce rate. Many spouses seek recognition as a person rather than as a husband, wife, mother, father, housekeeper, or breadwinner.

Second, this concept helps explain much of the intergenerational conflict. The parents of the 1960s and 1970s were reared in a society which said survival goals took precedence over role or identity. ("Son, I believe you ought to take the job even if it's not exactly what you want. You'll never find anything else that pays this much!") Their children have been reared in a world that says identity is more important than survival goals. ("Sorry, Dad, but I just couldn't be happy in that job, no matter how much it pays. It just isn't me. I want to do something that lets me express myself as a person, rather than simply make a lot of money.")

Third, as Glasser points out, in an identity-oriented society the important motivating forces are involvement and cooperation, not power. In a survival goal era power was the prime motivating force. Thus survival goal-minded teachers place a heavy emphasis on discipline, respect for authority, respect for position, and order. The identity-oriented teacher believes the best way to motivate identity-oriented people is by recognition as a person, participation, involvement, and cooperation. The classroom of the identity-oriented teacher rarely is as quiet or as orderly as the classroom of the survival goal-oriented teacher. This highly visible difference may be very distressing to the fifty-year-old teacher who was reared in a survival goal world but has been converted to identity-oriented adult.

Fourth, this shift from survival goals to an emphasis on identity and role is a threat to every institution which was founded in a survival goal era and which seeks to motivate and control people by power. Among the most threatened institutions in American society as a result of this shift are prisons, schools, black colleges, women's colleges, church-related schools, the armed forces, police departments, the Roman Catholic Church, the Lutheran Church-Missouri Synod, the traditional political organization which depended upon "clout" to win supporters, hospitals, and every other organization that still functions on the assumption that survival goals take precedence over the quest for identity.

Fifth, in both individual and organizational terms a focus on survival goals tends to produce a sense of unity while a focus on the quest for identity and fulfillment of role tends to be divisive. A national illustration of this can be seen by comparing the impact of World War II, a clear example of a survival goal, with the impact on the nation of the Vietnam conflict, which was perceived by some older leaders as a survival issue, but which most of the American people increasingly saw as concerned with the identity of the United States and this nation's role in world affairs.

Sixth, as is pointed out in chapter 10, the change is a basic reason why institutions no longer can depend on an inherited loyalty of members.

Finally, this change helps explain why it is important to examine the shift from an emphasis on the functional to an emphasis on the relational in our society.

4
From Functional
To Relational

The forty-year-old social studies teacher was reflecting on his eighteen years of teaching in the same junior high school. "About seven to ten years ago I began to realize that reinforcing self-image was a more important part of my job than was teaching content. When I began teaching the balance was probably 90 percent content and 10 percent concern for the kids as individuals. Today I guess it is at least 60 percent, maybe even 70 percent, building relationships with kids so I can be helpful to them as persons and no more than 30 or 40 percent concern with content."

In the early 1950s one of the popular predictions was that by 1975 children would not leave home to go to school for their education. They would stay home and be taught by master teachers on television.

Another parallel projection was that by 1975 the pulpit would be replaced in most Protestant churches by a giant television screen. Each week the congregation would have its choice of one of several great preachers to see and hear via television. Every pastor would receive early in the week a list of the sermons and preachers that would be available on television the following Sunday and make a choice from that list. The minister would act as the liturgist for the worship service, but this would save him ten to twenty hours of sermon preparation time every week and also provide every congregation with high quality preaching week after week.

A new chief executive officer is named for a corporation with $50 million in sales annually. Immediately on taking office, the executive reorganizes the company from an arrangement which had eight major divisions with three to six departments in each division to a new system in which there are four major division heads who report to him directly and each division consists of seven to twelve departments.

The pulpit search committee at the twenty-four-hundred-member Westminster Church was instructed by the governing body of the congregation to find a new minister who was an outstanding preacher and an excellent administrator. They were told repeatedly that it did not matter about his other qualifications as long as he could preach and administer a large congregation. They could hire other staff members to fill in where this new minister might be weak. The pulpit search committee took these instructions literally and found a minister who was an outstanding preacher and had an excellent reputation as an administrator. They recommended him to the congregation, he was called, and he accepted the call. Two years later another committee was appointed to call upon the new minister to encourage him to seek a call to another congregation.

"I must confess I cannot remember very much I ever learned in her classes, but that woman had more of an influence on my life than anyone I have ever known with the exception of my parents and my husband," remarked a thirty-five-year-old executive in a large corporation. "She taught biology, and I guess I could tell you all I know about biology in ten seconds, but it would take a couple of hours for me to explain how and why she had such a tremendous impact on my life."

"I know the prices are a little higher here than they are over at the supermarket," explained the housewife who had been asked why she drove five miles each way to buy her groceries at a family-run corner grocery store. "But when we first moved here we lived in an apartment two blocks west of this store and we did most of our shopping here. We got pretty well acquainted and when we bought our own home I just kept on coming back here. After all, it's nice to have people call you by name and to remember who you are."

"I never even thought of calling anyone else," replied the widow to her son-in-law when he asked why she called a particular funeral director. Her daughter, who was also the young man's wife, had been killed in an accident while visiting back home. "After all, Mr. Rogers buried both of my parents and my husband. I didn't know anyone else I could call."

A few years ago a high-school-age youth group from a church in Kentucky went up to spend a week in a work camp helping repair dilapidated housing in one of the slums of Detroit's inner city. That same week a group of young people from a church in suburban Detroit went down to Appalachia to help repair the house occupied by a family in which the husband and father had been totally disabled in a coal mining accident.

When they heard about this coincidence some of the parents in the suburban Detroit congregation wondered why their young people chose to go all the way down to Kentucky to "do good" when they could have done more good at less cost by spending that week working closer to home.

"My mother, who was born and spent all of her life in Wisconsin, used to ask me why I went way off to Tennessee to find a wife," remarked a young husband. "She couldn't understand why, with all of those pretty girls in Wisconsin, I couldn't find a wife closer to home rather than complicating life by going so far away to pick a bride. She felt it would have been simpler and cheaper to pick a girl closer to home. I tried to explain to her that those decisions aren't made on the basis of cold logic and a rational approach to the world."

These ten paragraphs illustrate a concept that is fundamental to understanding tomorrow. Increasingly the world is moving from an emphasis on the functional to placing a high priority on the relational dimensions of life. More and more people are willing to pay the costs that accompany an emphasis on the relational aspects of life.

The prediction that children would be educated at home in front of the television receiver completely overlooked the socialization processes that are an essential element of learning. The best teachers know this or learn it as the years ago by. The teachers who stand out in students' memories years later usually are remembered because of relationships, not because of scholarship. The best preaching is done by the minister who knows the members of the congregation and no television preacher can compete with that relationship.

When a new person is appointed as the chief executive officer of a large corporation he knows intuitively that one way to establish the necessary relationships between him and his chief subordinates is through a reorganization which helps everyone know that he owns the new table of organization.

The pulpit search committee at Westminster Church found a minister who excelled in preaching and administration, but his one-to-one relationships with parishioners left much to be desired and it soon became apparent that the real priority was a minister who could relate to the members individually as well as collectively.

Whether it be the choice of a grocer, a physician, a mortician, or a wife, people usually place a premium on interpersonal relationships rather than on economic, geographical, or professional criteria.

When a group of high school students go out to spend a week repairing dilapidated homes the primary thrust is on relationships, both within the group and between the group and people in another subculture. Functional, economic, and efficiency considerations are a distant second!

What Are the Implications?

The implications and consequences of this growing emphasis on the relational dimensions of life are too many to review here, but it may help to lift up several.

1. This concept is of basic importance to financing voluntary associations. The higher the level of trust between the members or constituents and the organization,

the more freely and generously will the people contribute funds to support that organization.

Another example of this concept can be seen in the financial support of the missionary efforts of the Protestant churches. Church members give more generously and with fewer reservations to projects or programs to which they can feel a relationship, perhaps through persons staffing the program or perhaps through the content of the program, than to such abstract concepts as "World Service," "Cooperative Program," "Church Finance Council," or "General Assembly Causes."

2. There is a basic tendency for lay people to think in relational terms, while professionals tend to think in functional terms. Therefore the seventy-three-year-old woman with a serious illness postpones going to see a specialist because she feels more comfortable going to see her family doctor who repeatedly has urged her to see a specialist. She keeps coming back to him until he takes her to the specialist.

Likewise clergy tend to think in functional terms so most congregations are organized formally by functional committees and informally by relational groupings of people, but for many of the laity these relational groups are far more important and meaningful than the functional boards and committees.

3. This concept helps explain why every effective organization has to have a leader who is oriented to functional concerns, to getting the job done, *and* a leader who is sensitive and responsive to the relationships to and among people.

4. This concept helps explain the choice of the "anchor team" on the television newscast and the choice of the person to report the weather. Frequently this is a place

to strengthen the relationships between the viewer and the announcer and also the viewer and that station.

5. This concept also helps to explain the hostility of people toward computers. A computer is the extreme example of the emphasis on the functional dimensions of life and people are looking for relationships not functional efficiency!

6. This shift from functional to relational is one of the reasons why an increasing number of ministers are being addressed either by the term "pastor" or by their first name rather than as "preacher" or "doctor."

7. This concept also offers a frame of reference for understanding some of the conflicts between the national staff of a voluntary association (service clubs, women's organizations in the churches, Scouting, professional societies, etc.) and the members of the local chapters. Frequently the national officers and staff, who often think in functional terms, clash on priorities, organizational structure, nomenclature, and expectations with the members of the local unit, many of whom are more concerned with relationships than with functions.

8. One of the less obvious consequences of this shift will be the growing pressures for individuals in person-centered jobs, where the strength of the trust relationship is important, to move less frequently. This category includes city managers, social workers, pastors, counselors, and editors.

9. Finally, this shift from the functional to the relational clearly is a factor in the rise in the divorce rate. Forty years ago many marriages were held together largely because of functional reasons (to provide a home for the children, the farmer needed a helper, etc.). Today the functional glue is inadequate.

The shift from a primary emphasis on survival goals to a primary emphasis on identity described in the previous chapter is a part of this changing context of American society. When taken together the contents of these two chapters help explain why tomorrow will bring an even greater emphasis on identity and the relational aspects of life.

These two concepts, along with the Big Revolution and the reverse civilizing process that began in the 1960s also provide part of the foundation for understanding why people's expectations of institutions usually exceed the performance.

5
Excessive Expectations Of Institutions

Through the years the American people have entrusted tremendous responsibilities to the institutions of society. The charitable impulse is increasingly channeled through a variety of philanthropic and benevolent organizations. The Congress and the President have turned over to the Department of Defense the basic authority over what were, until the Key West Agreement of 1947, the very competitive branches of the armed forces. Many people find identity in their involvement in institutions, and for others institutions offer an opportunity for them to express themselves.

To a very substantial degree people have turned responsibility over to two institutions, the schools and the churches, to cause children to grow up the way the parents want them to turn out as adults. And to a very substantial degree the results of research over the past decade suggest that these and other expectations placed on institutions far exceed their capabilities. The first major blast came with the publication in 1966 of the study of Peter Rossi and Andrew Greeley which demonstrated the remarkably weak influence of Catholic education on the religious practices of adults who had been educated in parochial schools.[1] Since that date scores of other studies by social scientists such as James Coleman, Christopher Jencks, Leonard J. Kogan, and others have documented the same basic point. Regardless of how much money they have to spend on staff and program there is a ceiling on what the schools and churches can do to influence the behavior patterns as the child grows to adulthood—and it is a much lower ceiling than most people are willing to admit.

Basically the research all comes out at the same point. The three most important factors which have a long term influence on the behavior pattern of an individual are the home, the community, and the one-to-one model.

For most people this list consists of only the home and one-to-one models since the word "community" here is used in a very narrow sense. As used here, the word community refers to a social group in which the members share several common characteristics, reside in a specific locality, and have a common cultural and historical heritage. Examples of such communities would include the German Lutheran farming community in Wisconsin in the 1920s, the Amish community in northeastern Ohio today, the Chinese-American community in San Francisco in the 1950s, or the Russian-Jewish neighborhood in New York City in the 1920s. In these and similar communities, social pressures clearly influence the behavior patterns of many of the people who are reared in these closely knit social groups.

The three immigrant groups and their descendants who rank highest on the socio-economic-educational scale—Chinese-Americans, Japanese-Americans, and Jewish-Americans—suggest that the tightly knit community can be very influential in the development of children.

Most people in the United States, however, do not live in this type of community and therefore the prime responsibility for influencing children appears to rest on the home and on the one-to-one model.

This position has been and continues to be vigorously resisted by many who insist that greater responsibility must be placed on the schools and the churches to produce a strong favorable influence on children. Two examples will illustrate this point. A large number of black and Hispanic parents are demanding that schools teach the basic skills which will prepare their children for jobs and for college. In the 1960s many of these parents were silent in the face of the demands of the white, liberal, upper-middle class parents who supported the new math and other innovations in educational practices, but now these black and Hispanic parents are demanding a greater emphasis on basic skills. While the evidence is overwhelming that the best way to cause a child to be competent in reading and to enjoy reading is to have that child grow up in a home where the parents and siblings spend considerable time reading and there are a variety of books and magazines in the home, the demand continues to grow that the schools should teach reading skills more effectively.

A second example can be found in the St. Louis suburb **of Clayton, Missouri, which at $2,650 has that state's** highest annual per pupil expenditure for the public schools. In an effort to be more effective in meeting the educational needs of the children a proposal has been developed for a comprehensive, home-based, school-administrated early childhood educational program for infants, one-year-olds, two-year-olds, and three-year-olds.

These two examples illustrate three of the most common slogans, "The schools should do it," "If the schools are going to do it they have to have more money," and "The schools cannot be expected to do it unless they have contact with the child earlier in life."

Similarly churches are expected to inculcate high moral standards, build character, and cause the child to grow up to be a committed Christian. Again the record shows that the surest way to have a child grow up to be an active church member is for that child to be reared in a home where both parents are active church members.

A parrallel story about the excessive expectations of institutions also could be told about the League of Nations, the United Nations, the Boy Scouts of America, the American Red Cross, the armed forces, the Republican Party, municipal government, colleges and universities, the American Medical Association, labor unions, and scores of other institutions. Anyone seeking to understand the future should reflect on this gap between expectations and performance as people view the institutions of society.

What Are the Implications?

The most obvious implication is that a burden has been placed on the schools, churches, and other institutions beyond their capability and a self-defeating cycle has been established.

Closely related to this is the widespread disillusionment with the larger institutions of our society documented in chapter 10. One result of this disillusionment is that institutions and organizations no longer can depend on the loyalty of members and potential members to be passed on from generation to generation.

A more subtle implication is that more attention should be given to the one-to-one model concept. The research evidence is very persuasive that children and youth are strongly influenced by adult models. Thus one of the most persuasive arguments for increasing the number of black or Hispanic or women newscasters, weather reporters, and commentators on television is to provide additional models for girls, for black children, and for **Spanish surnamed youth. It may be that as this concept** gains more widespread recognition it will change the shape of many organizations.

This concept and the effect it might have on an organization can be illustrated by looking at the youth fellowship groups in the churches. For decades the usual concept was to organize a youth group with either (a) the minister of youth work responsible for it if that congregation could afford to hire a youth minister or (b) an adult couple "in charge" as counselors. This arrangement tended to focus attention on questions as these.

Question. How do we evaluate the effectiveness of this part of the church program?

Answer. First, the bigger the better; the more youth who are actively involved, the more effective that program. Second, the larger the proportion of young people who come out of the youth group into active church membership as adults, the better the program.

Question. What are the most important issues that should receive attention as ministers, parents, youth workers, and church leaders discuss the youth program?

Answer. The most important issues include the role of the leaders, the program or activities of the group, the organization of the group and how the leaders are to be selected, the number who are actively involved, why certain young people are reluctant to participate, the right age range to be included in any one group, and the relationship of the youth program to other programs of the church.

Contrast this set of questions and answers with what

happens when the youth fellowship is organized using the one-to-one model concept. In this approach a basic reason for the existence of the junior high youth fellowship is to expose these young people to several different models of an adult Christian and to provide opportunities for these youth to interact with them. The typical approach is one adult counselor for every two youth active in the group.

Among the questions aroused by this approach are these: What do we, as leaders of this congregation, believe are the distinctive characteristics of an adult Christian the youth should be exposed to? Why do we lift up these characteristics as the most important? Who in our congregation best exemplify these characteristics? If youth are primarily concerned with questions of identity rather than with survival goals (chap. 3), will these adults be able to relate to youth and will youth see them as desirable models? Are we more concerned with what the youth will do or with the relationships that will be formed? Are we more concerned with causing the youth to be active church members or with encouraging them to have a depth relationship with people we see as models of an adult Christian?

Finally, as the focus of American society continues to shift from an effort to train young people to grow up to become good loyal members and supporters of the existing institutions and organizations of society to helping young people discover who they are, to realize their own God-given gifts and potential, and to develop the institutions and organizations that their new society will need, this shift requires any future-oriented individual to be aware of the shift from the verbal to the visual in communication and education.

6
From The Verbal To The Visual

It was the first Sunday in October and the twelve-year-old boy came into the Sunday school class for fifth- and sixth-graders at Trinity Church a few minutes after the class had started. It was obvious, simply by looking at him, that he was a newcomer and that probably his parents had come to Trinity for the first time that Sunday. As they went their way they probably said, "Jimmy, go find the sixth-grade class and meet us right here when you're through."

The next Sunday Jimmy was there when the class started. The third Sunday in October he was at the door waiting when the teacher arrived, about fifteen minutes early, to arrange the room for that day's class. The fourth Sunday Jimmy also was there early and as he helped the teacher arrange the room, he asked in a timid voice, "Don't you ever sit around in a big circle and go blah-blah?"

The teacher replied, "Why, yes, we do occasionally bring everyone together to talk over what we're all doing and to discuss anything that requires everyone's attention, but I guess we haven't done that since you joined us."

"Where we lived before, all we ever did in Sunday school was sit around in a big circle and go blah-blah-blah," replied Jimmy, "and I hated it!"

That fall Jimmy's class at Trinity Church was studying

the history of the early Christian church. As a major part of the learning process they made an 8-millimeter motion picture with sound of the burning of Rome and the early Christians going underground. One group of students researched the story of the burning of Rome and of the early Christians meeting in the catacombs and wrote the script. Another group did the research necessary to find or build the sets. Another group took the script and cast the characters for their parts. A fifth-grade boy served as cinematographer and some other boys built a model of a monastery to demonstrate a later era in the history of Christianity.

This class used both verbal skills and visual skills in studying the history of the early church. What they also were doing was demonstrating a major change in our society. This is the shift from a culture which trained people to function around verbal skills, and placed a very high reward on competence in verbal skills, to a society which is placing an increasing emphasis on visual skills in communication and education. This is a basic concept that is essential to an understanding of what tomorrow will bring.

Most early written languages were, like Chinese of today, essentially picture writing. When the Phoenicians invented the phonetic alphabet they provided an alphabet that could be adapted, with minor modifications, to almost any language. The Western world, for example, has had to add only three letters, *u, w,* and *j,* to the alphabet that was sufficient for the Romans—and the *j* and the *u* were not added until about three hundred years ago.

The results of the evolution of the alphabet and of centuries of emphasizing verbal-auditory channels for the communication of the English language and for learning are worth reflecting on for a moment.

First, we have an alphabet that was very well suited to Latin and made it fit another language. The result is a poor fit and a language that is difficult to speak and very, very difficult to write or read. A good phonetic alphabet must have one sound for each letter and one letter for each sound. Our alphabet has eight different sounds for the first letter of the alphabet!

Second, thanks to Noah Webster and others, the attempts to standardize spelling by creating a right and a wrong way to spell a word have wiped out two of the great advantages of a phonetic alphabet. In a phonetic alphabet words *should* be spelled as they sound, not as some writer of spelling books declares they should be spelled. In addition we now have been taught that it is correct that words should be spelled one way and pronounced another. Thus was eliminated the chance to standardize the spoken language with the writtten word. As a result these these two basic means of communicating, the written word and the spoken word, have been drifting apart.

Third, we have made communication by the written word a chore that most people find to be difficult, tiring, boring, and frustrating.

Fourth, and this is a relatively recent discovery, it appears that verbal-auditory language skills develop in the left hemisphere of the brain and that visual skills develop in the right hemisphere of the brain.

Fifth, the evidence strongly suggests that the preschool experiences of most children tend to emphasize the development of visual skills and this tendency has been strongly reinforced by television. (Television appeals primarily to the right hemisphere of the brain.)

Sixth, while the data supporting this generalization are somewhat inconclusive, it appears that males have more difficulty developing the left hemisphere of the brain than do females and one result is that boys are more likely to have problems in developing verbal skills than are girls. This may be why television tends to appeal more to boys than to girls.

Seventh, research by Dr. Gene Symes of the National Institute for Mental Health suggests that frequently young boys who have trouble reading (most grade school students who have reading difficulties are boys) are predisposed toward visual thinking. In general, the better they were able to conceptualize visually, the more likely they would have reading difficulties.

Eighth, the median test score on verbal ability administered by the College Entrance Examination Board fell from 478 in 1962–63 to 434 for 1973–74.

Ninth, if a boy has a natural tendency toward use of visual skills and the first seven or eight or nine years of his life are spent helping him develop the right hemisphere of his brain and he spends several hours every day watching television, is it surprising that he has difficulty in verbal skills, which are developed in the left hemisphere of the brain, when he reaches third grade? Why should anyone expect this boy to easily master verbal skills when the alphabet on which they are based tends to make the spoken word unlike the written word? Why should he be expected to excel in reading when the alphabet used is one which tends to make reading difficult, boring, tiresome, and frustrating?

Tenth, more and more schools are providing increased opportunities for students to express themselves by the use of visual skills and are finding this reinforces the student's self-esteem. The progression in skill development is from visual to oral to written forms of communication.

What Are the Implications?

1. The basic implication of this is that we are living in a world in which people born before 1950 have been trained to place a premium on competence in verbal skills and a substantial proportion of the people born after 1950 have been conditioned by television to believe that the world functions around visual skills.

2. The communications training informally taught small children in the home often accentuates visual skills while the communications training taught in the public schools emphasizes verbal skills—and probably confuses many young boys.

3. The adult Sunday school teacher who enjoys reading and who has a high level of competence in verbal skills probably will try to conduct class using verbal skills as the basic channel of communication. If this is a new class composed of adult women, the natural informal selection process used in determining membership in this new class probably will result in what everyone evaluates as a good learning expeirence. If, however, this individual is asked to teach a class of third grade children between one-third and one-half of the boys in the class will be bored and many will misbehave.

4. If this is a culture which is moving from an emphasis on verbal skills to an acceptance of visual skills as a "legitimate" form of communication, every teaching situation either will (a) segregate the visual skill-oriented people from the verbal skill-oriented people or (b) cause at least some of the people to be bored during the entire experience.

5. The people who will be the most effective teachers in a situation using visual skills as the primary channel of communication probably will not be persons who enjoy sitting around reading for hours at a time.

6. Most of the severe critics of television are verbal skill-oriented individuals who have difficulty comprehending how some people function primarily around visual skills.

These half dozen comments represent only the tip of the iceberg in any discussion of the implications of this shift from the verbal to the visual, but they should be sufficient to persuade the reader that this trend is of fundamental importance in understanding tomorrow.

7
The Missing 700,000

Everyone is aware of the impact of the post-World War II "baby boom" on American society. For fifty years the number of babies born in the United States ranged between 2.3 and 3.1 million each year, only twice reaching the 3 million level, in 1921 and in 1943. In twenty-four of the thirty-seven years between 1909 and 1945 that total was between 2.7 and 2.9 million births annually.

In 1946, however, the number of babies born was up 25 percent over the previous year and the total continued to climb until it passed 4 million in 1954, and it was not until 1965 that the total number of live births dropped below that 4 million level. In five of those eleven years more than 4.2 million babies were born. The impact of the Pill brought an 8 percent drop to 3,760,000 births in 1965, and it appeared that the bottom had been reached in 1968 when only 3.5 million live births were recorded.

By 1969 the children born in the first years of the post–World War II baby boom were now old enough to become parents in sufficient numbers to move the total back up to 3.6 million births. The probability that this was a trend in a new direction was verified in 1970 when the total number of live births climbed to 3.73 million. It was obvious to anyone who could count that the number of babies born each year would continue to rise as more and more of the babies born back in the

1943–64 era moved into the ranks of parenthood. Projections based on the number of people born in the 1950s and early 1960s and the number of marriages entered into each year indicated that by 1975 the total number of births would reach 4.2 million and probably pass the 4.5 million mark by 1980. The number of marriages, which peaked at 2.3 million in 1946, dropped to 1.6 million in 1949, and then leveled off in the 1.5 to 1.6 million range between 1951 and 1963. In a very predictable trend, the number of marriages began to climb upward, to 1.8 million in 1965, to 2.2 million in 1971 and on up to 2.28 million in 1973 before dropping slightly in 1974 to 2.2 million. Even after allowing for the impact of the Pill and the preference for smaller families, it was obvious that the mid-1970s would bring a return to a plateau of births in the 4 to 4.5 million total each year.

But something went wrong with the "facts" behind these projections!

The number of babies born in 1971 totaled only 3,559,000, down 4.6 percent from the 1970 total, and the 1972 total was down 8.5 percent from that 1971 figure. Instead of a continued increase, there was a 13 percent drop in two years! In 1972, for the first time in American history, "the total fertility rate," the measurement for predicting long-term population trends, dropped below zero population growth. On a long term basis, births were not sufficient to offset deaths. By 1974 the total fertility rate had dropped to 1.86. (This means that the average woman would bear 1.86 children during her lifetime. An average rate of 2.11 children per adult woman is necessary to maintain a stable population.)

The number of babies born each year continued to diminish, rather than rise and the total for 1973 was slightly under 3.2 million and that figure went up only one percent in 1974.

What happened?

Instead of an expected 3.9 to 4.2 million babies being born each year during the middle 1970s, the total hovered in the 3.2 to 3.4 million range.

This means that each year an expected 700,000 babies are not being born. (There is some evidence to suggest that the long-awaited "baby boom of the 1970s" began in 1974–1975 and that by 1979 this "deficit" in births will be down to 300,000 babies.)

This is one of the most significant numbers to be remembered by the person who seeks to understand what tomorrow will bring. These 700,000 babies who were not born each year during the middle 1970s already are making their impact felt in several ways. It may be helpful to look at a few of these implications and consequences.

What Are the Implications?

The nominating committee at University Church was meeting to prepare for the once-a-year ritual of recommending who should be elected to the various leadership positions for the coming year. Among the seven members of the committee was fifty-one-year-old Walter Sullivan of the Sociology Department of the University.

When the committee reached the point that they were beginning to list names for the Board of Christian Education someone suggested Joan Wickert and Lois Brown.

"When were Joan and Lois born?" inquired Professor Sullivan in a mild voice.

"I'm not sure," responded Sue Adams. "Let's see now, Joan and my husband were in school together so I guess she was born in about 1933, and Lois is a few years younger so I guess she was born in about 1936 or 1937. Why? What difference does that make?"

"It makes all the difference in the world," replied Walter Sullivan. "If you are correct in your estimates of their birth year, or even close, I would oppose nominating either one of them for the Board of Christian Education or for any other policy-making group. They are a part of the most atypical age cohort in the adult population, and I don't believe we should recommend any woman born in the 1930s for a policy-making position. Everyone of us is tempted to project our own perspective or view of reality and to impose our own experiences and value systems on others. We can't prevent people from doing that, but we can avoid increasing the tensions produced by that tendency by not putting any women born in the 1930s on any policy making board here at University Church."

"Walter, I had never thought of this before," interrupted Agnes Peterson, "but you not only look like a fat male chauvinist pig, you also sound like one!"

"Go on, tell us more. Explain what you mean," urged Gene Winkler. "My wife also was born in the 1930s."

"Please don't misunderstand me," protested Professor Sullivan. "There's nothing personal in what I'm saying. It simply is a fact that women born in the 1930s represent a very unusual group in our population. They were born when the birth rate was at the lowest point it had ever been up to that time, they married younger than any other age cohort of women before or since, they set a modern record for the size of their families and a larger proportion of women born in the 1930s married than any other age group. Demographers predict that at least 96 percent of the women born in the 1930s will marry at least once. It also appears that they will set a record for the smallest proportion of childless women in any age group in our nation's history since at least 90 percent of them, regardless of marital status, will give birth to at least one child. It has been easier for this group of women than for any previous group to combine a husband, a family, and a job outside the home. Women in this age group with one or more years of graduate school hold the record among all groups of women for the highest proportion who are divorced (7.3 percent in 1970), while women in this age group who terminated their education after four years of college hold the record for the smallest proportion who are divorced (3.9 percent in 1970)." As it appeared he was about to conclude his analysis members of the committee began to speak at once.

"Allow me one more minute, please," pleaded Professor Sullivan. "All I am saying is that women born in the 1930s are more unlike the generation of women both in the decade before them *and* the generation born after them than any other age cohort. I am simply suggesting that we be conscious of this fact when we recommend persons for a committee or board where they will be making policy for parents and children, most of whom were born in a later era."

While some readers, especially women born in the 1930s, may disagree with Professor Sullivan's conclusion that women born during the Great Depression should not be in policy-making positions, his facts are accurate. One result of the combination of factors that produced the birth dearth of the 1970s is that women born during the 1930s are unlike either the generation of women born before them in the 1920s and also unlike the generation of women born during the 1940s.

A second set of consequences of the 700,000 babies currently not being born each year has been widely publicized in the public press. These consequences include the closing of the maternity wing in many hospitals, the surplus of elementary school rooms and teachers, empty nurseries in church school buildings, and the diversification of companies that formerly specialized in producing products for the baby market. (Gerber Products Co. used to advertise "Babies are our only business." They have dropped the word "only" from that slogan.)

The drop in births caused the Bureau of the Census to add another line to their annual projection of population growth. Traditionally the bureau issued a set of four projections A, B, C, and D. Beginning in 1973, however, they added an E series which was based on a projection of 1.8 children per family. This projection produces a population of 250 million in the United States for the year 2000 compared to 217 million in 1976.

If the fertility rate remains at 1.80 this will mean 3.7 million births in 1985, if it climbs to 2.1 (zero population growth), 1985 will see 4.3 million babies born in the United States. If the girls born in the 1960s have children at the rate their mothers who were born in the 1930s gave birth, this would mean more than 6 million babies would be born in 1990!

Many of the most interesting consequences of this will be felt by the babies who were born in the 1970s. In order to fill those empty classrooms, to employ those teachers who otherwise would not have jobs, and to keep the school administrators busy, children born in the 1970s probably will start school younger and spend more days per year in school than any previous generation (see chap. 11).

Many years hence these babies who were born in the 1970s will miss their brothers and sisters who were not born. They will miss them when it comes to voting on pensions and increases in Social Security payments in the year 2020 (see chap. 16), they will miss them in the first decade of the next century when it comes to staffing all of the organizations which depend on youthful volunteers, they will miss them if and when the United States becomes involved in a major war in the late 1980s or early 1990s (wars are fought largely with persons in the 17–25 age group), and they will miss them when it comes to filling up all of the church buildings constructed in the 1950s and 1960s. It is possible that the babies born during the 1970s will miss those children who were not born to the extent that the large family will become popular again around the turn of the century.

Another consequence is that a society which for a quarter of a century was heavily oriented toward children and youth will become increasingly oriented toward mature adults.

One of the important beneficiaries will be women born between 1962 and 1968. Since women usually marry men who are a year or two or three older, this means that women born in this period will have a disproportionately large number of men to choose from. Their situation will be the opposite of that of women born in the 1945–57 period when the number of births was on the increase. Those women found themselves in a market which was short of single men a few years older than themselves.

Finally, the birth dearth of the 1970s may reverse the divorce rate which climbed sharply in the early

1970s. There are two reasons for suggesting this. First, fewer marriages are being entered into because the woman is pregnant. Second, according to a study by the Institute for Social Research of the University of Michigan, the happiest people are childless married couples. The unhappiest are those who are divorced or separated followed by widows and the third unhappiest group are single adults who never married. The second most happy are the couples whose children are grown. As the number of childless couples increases and as the number of families with only one or two children increases, the happiness rate may go up and the divorce rate may come down. Maybe!

To look at the missing 700,000 is to see only one side of the population growth pattern. To more adequately understand tomorrow it is necessary also to look at the new immigration.

8

The New Immigration

"No Swedish Pastor will come after me, since the descendants of the old colonies no longer speak the Swedish language. No immigration from Sweden can be of any great importance and should be discouraged, which I have done during thirty years through letters to many persons in Sweden." [1]

When Pastor Nils Collins wrote this on May 12, 1823, fewer than 30 thousand Swedes had migrated to the United States, and the population of Sweden was slightly over 3 million. During the next century more than three-quarters of a million Swedes came to the United States, and the population of Sweden more than doubled. Pastor Collins, like millions of people before and after him, looked out at the world and concluded that the major changes were behind him when actually even greater changes lay in the future.

This same attitude has marked the American view toward immigration for sixty years.

In numerical terms there have been six big waves of immigrants into the United States, all of them since Pastor Collins' letter was written. The first began in 1845 when 120,000 immigrants arrived on these shores, and this wave peaked in 1954 when 461,000 arrived. The coming of the Civil War slowed the pace, and the second big wave occurred in the 1863–1875 era when an average of 300,000 immigrants entered this country each year. The third big wave of immigration into the United States began in 1880 when the number of immigrants entering the United States totaled 457,257, up from 177,826 in 1879. The peak of this wave came in 1907 when 1,285,349 were recorded by the immigration authorities. In thirteen different years, 1882 and 1903 through 1914, at least 750,000 new Americans arrived during each twelve-month period and on five occasions the total topped a million.

A short-lived fourth wave followed the close of World War I and peaked at 805,228 in 1921. Legislation enacted in 1924, which specifically favored white, Anglo-Saxon, northern European immigrants halted that wave which came largely from southern and eastern Europe.

In 1933 only 23,068 immigrants came to the United States, the lowest figure recorded since 1827. From 1932 through 1945 that annual figure never climbed above 83,000 and in nine of those fourteen years was below 40,000. An interesting facet of the immigration during the 1930–1950 era is that women outnumbered men among the immigrants by a 3 to 2 margin, exactly the opposite of the pattern for the previous hundred years.

A fifth wave peaked in 1956 and 1957, and it is worth noting that of the 326,867 immigrants who arrived in 1959, over one-half came from Europe (including 60,353 from Germany), 49,321 from Mexico, 46,354 from Canada and Newfoundland, and only 20,000 from all of Asia. Well over one-half of these newcomers in 1957 came from the British Isles, northern Europe, Germany, Scandanavia, and Canada. Most Americans could look at them and say, "They're like us."

The sixth and current big wave is numerically the second largest of these six waves of immigration. In size it is topped only by the 1880–1914 period during which 22 million newcomers landed here.

The size, and especially the composition of this new immigration, is important for anyone seeking to understand tomorrow. Thanks to a little-publicized 1965 law that abolished the "national origins" quota system that had restricted immigration for four decades, this new wave opened the doors to a different part of the world.

For comparison purposes it may be helpful to look at the source of the immigration for four different years.

SOURCES OF IMMIGRATION INTO UNITED STATES

	1882	1914	1957	1973
Percent from Europe	82%	88%	52%	23%
Great Britain	13	4	8	3
Ireland	9	2	3	0.4
Scandinavia	13	2	2	0.4
Germany	32	3	19	2
Italy	4	24	6	5
Central & Eastern	6	46	5	1
Percent from Asia	5	3	6	30
China	5	0.2	0.6	2
Percent from Canada	12	7	14	4
Percent from Mexico	0.05	1	15	18
Percent from Central and South America	0.2	2	12	23
Percent from Africa	0	1	1	1

In sixty years the immigrants from Europe have dropped from nine-tenths of the total to less than one-fourth. Sixty years ago one-half of the immigrants came from central and eastern Europe (this was the source of the large Jewish immigration of the first part of this century) and another quarter came from southern Europe.

Today the largest sources are "south of the border"— Mexico, Central America, South America, and the islands in the Caribbean—and Asia. In 1965 immigrants from southern Asia and the Far East accounted for 5 percent of all newcomers legally admitted to the United States, but by 1974 this porportion had jumped to 29 percent as a result of the 1965 legislation. For the decade of 1965 to 1974, 210,000 Filipinos came to the United States along with 112,000 Koreans and 147,000 from China and Taiwan. In addition there were 86,000 immigrants from India, 42,000 from Japan, and 40,000 from Hong Kong.

While the final figures for 1975 are not available at this writing, it appears that nearly one-half of the estimated 550,000 immigrants coming into the United States in 1975 will be from southern Asia and the Far East. The 1974 legal immigration from Mexico was 71,586, nearly double the total of the decade earlier. Immigration from the West Indies has climbed from 25,330 in 1970 to over 60,000 in 1974.

What Are the Implications?

The implications of this new immigration are of basic importance for an understanding of tomorrow and the far-reaching consequences can be illustrated by looking at several dimensions of what is happening.

The most obvious implication of the new immigration is the change in the source of population growth in the

United States. During the 1950s, for example, the population of this nation increased by 28 million persons. Approximately 25 million of this increase, or 90 percent, was a result of births exceeding deaths by an annual average of 2.5 million.

During the 1960s the population increased by 24.2 million and births exceeded deaths by an average of only 2 million per year. Net civilian immigration accounted for 16 percent of the total increase compared to only 10 percent of the 1950s and 8 percent of the net increase of the 1940s.

During the 1970s it is expected that births will exceed deaths by approximately 16 million (36 million births during the decade minus 20 million deaths) and the net civilian migration will total 5 million including refugees, but excluding the illegal immigrants who probably will number another 5 million. Thus immigration, legal and illegal, will account for nearly 40 percent of the actual population growth of the 1970s.

A second facet of the impact of this new wave of immigration can be described best by referring to the first page of the *Kerner Report* issued by the National Advisory Commission on Civil Disorders published in early 1968. Perhaps the most widely quoted phrase from that report was the basic conclusion, "Our nation is moving toward two societies, one black, one white—separate and unequal."

In 1968, the year the report was published, the number of legal immigrants into the United States was reported at 454,448, up 26 percent from the total of a year earlier. Approximately 180,000 or 40 percent of that year's immigrants (excluding Spanish-speaking Puerto Ricans coming to the mainland) came from countries where Spanish is the national language. By 1975 well over one-half of the immigrants, both legal and illegal, spoke Spanish as their native language. According to some estimates, which place the illegal immigration much higher, the Spanish-speaking newcomers may have accounted for close to two-thirds of all immigrants in 1975 despite the addition of 150,000 Vietnamese and Cambodian refugees the total for that year.

The new immigration, assisted by the flight of tens of thousands of Cuban refugees, was making that famous quotation from the Kerner Report obsolete the year it was written. In 1968 the United States was moving toward three societies, one white and largely English-speaking, one black and native-born, and one Spanish-speaking. Probably by 1990, perhaps sooner, and almost certainly by 2000, the Hispanic Americans will outnumber the Afro-Americans and become the second largest of these three societies on the American scene.

Depending on the measures taken to stem the flood of illegal immigration, the day when Spanish-speaking people will outnumber American-born blacks in the United States may come even sooner than 1990. The Bureau of the Census reported that in March 1974 there were 10.8 million residents of Spanish origin in the United States of whom 6.4 million (60 percent) were of Mexican origin, 1.5 million (14 percent) Puerto Ricans, 0.7 million (6 percent) Cubans, and 0.7 million (6 percent) from Central or South America. A few months later in November 1974 Leonard F. Chapman, Jr., Commissioner of the United States Immigration and Naturalization Service, stated that the "illegal alien population in the United States numbers at least 6 or 7 million, and is possibly as great as 10 or 12 million."

The vast majority of illegal aliens in the United States are Spanish-speaking persons although there is a sizable minority from Asia.

For comparison purposes the Bureau of the Census reported the 1974 Negro population of the United States at 24 million, although the "undercount" which definitely failed to include many blacks in the census may add another 4 or 5 million to that total. For purposes of political analysis it is worth noting that in the 1972 general elections 44 percent of the eligible Spanish-surnamed citizens were registered to vote compared with 68 percent of the eligible black citizens and 73 percent of the "Anglo" population.

A third facet of what is happening as a result of the new immigration can be seen by looking at professional baseball. When Jackie Robinson broke the color bar in major league baseball he was followed by scores of other American Negroes. Black children had new models of what they could aspire to as they watched Robinson, Willie Mays, Reggie Jackson, Hank Aaron, Vida Blue, Dick Allen, Lou Brock, Frank Robinson, Ernie Banks, Maury Wills, Willie Stargell, Billy Williams, Larry Doby, Monte Irvin, Willie McCovey, and Bob Gibson break old records and set new ones. Black players began to gain a large share of the headlines, and many sports analysts attributed the superiority of the National League over the American League to the latter's delay in signing black players in the late 1940s and the 1950s.

In recent years the picture has changed and a growing proportion of the baseball stars are players born and reared in the Caribbean, Mexico, Central and South America. They include such stars as the Alou brothers— Felipe, Jesus, and Matty— plus Rico Carty, Cesar Cedino, and Juan Marichal from the Dominican Republic; Luis **Aparicio and Dave Concepcion from Venezuela; Rod** Carew and Manny Sanguillen from Panama; and Jose Cardinal, Tony Perez, Bert Campaneris, Luis Tiant, Cesar Tovar, Tony Oliva, and Mike Cuellar from Cuba. While they are not immigrants since Puerto Rico is a part of the United States, this list of baseball stars with a Latin background must be expanded to include Puerto Ricans such as Roberto Clemente, Vic Power, Orlando Cepeda, and Juan Pizarro.

More significant than the past, however, is the future. A survey of the top minor league prospects in mid-1975 revealed that American Negroes are outnumbered by the top Latin prospects from Central and South America and the Caribbean Islands including Puerto Rico, and blacks account for only 15 percent of the top minor league prospects. It appears that as the American-born black players dominated the national pastime during the third quarter of this century, the stars of the future are a part of this new immigration.

A fourth facet of the new immigration can be seen in the Roman Catholic Church which for more than a century in the United States has been dominated by Irish Catholics. Today the Irish account for only one-sixth of the total number of Catholics in the United States, and both the Italian Catholics and the Polish Catholics are outnumbered by Hispanic Catholics, who constitute the largest ethnic group in the Roman Catholic Church in the United States.

A fifth example of the impact of the new immigration is the emergence of large new ethnic pockets all across the continent. These include 175,000 Haitians in New York City, an estimated 30,000 Samoans in Los Angeles, an uncounted number of Koreans in Toronto, and close to a million Mexican-Americans in Chicago. There also are very large Mexican-American communities in Newark, El Paso, Austin, Phoenix, Los Angeles, Dallas, San Antonio, Denver, and New York.

As the years pass these will become very important power blocs in the political scene in scores of cities. An introduction to tomorrow can be found in Miami today.

A sixth and very significant dimension of this new immigration is that it is enlarging the numbers and sharply lowering the median age of many of the long established ethnic or nationality neighborhoods in several cities. In New York City, for example, in 1965 Chinatown was an aging community with between 30,000 and 40,000 residents of Chinese ancestry. Ten years later there were close to 100,000 Chinese in New York. The same pattern can be observed in literally hundreds of other cities where the Mexican-American, Chinese, Greek, Portuguese, Cambodian, East Indian, Japanese, Filipino, Korean, Vietnamese, Cuban, West Indian, or Haitian community is larger, younger, and far more militant than it was in the early 1960s.

A seventh facet of the new immigration which has far-reaching implications concerns the churches and other voluntary associations which have moved increasingly toward a policy of the "Americanization" of all members and participants of those organizations. This policy, which more accurately can be described as a "white, middle-class, homogenizing process," can be illustrated by looking at the churches. The churches have adopted and implemented this homogenizing process through a variety of means including the seminary training of ministers, creation of regional judicatories on a geographical basis rather than by recognition of ethnic characteristics, denominational mergers, bureaucratic restructuring efforts, insisting on English as the official language at all regional and national church conventions, scheduling meetings of the regional and national agencies of the denomination for the convenience of clergy and other upper-middle and upper class members rather than to maximize the participation of the working class, coopting indigenous lay and clergy leadership from the ethnic churches for regional and national church positions, and the use of standardized resources for worship, Christian education, and membership training.

To a substantial extent the growing religious bodies of the next dozen years will be those religious bodies which affirm the legitimacy of the ethnic church, which encourage a bilingual approach to preaching the Word, which are able to affirm a pluralistic style of church life, and which are not locked in to exclusionary procedures on the ordination of ministers, the recognition and acceptance of ethnic congregations, and the involvement of laity in the ongoing life of the denominational family.

Another dimension of the impact of the new immigration will become increasingly apparent in the public schools. Should the young children of these newcomers be educated in a format which treats English as a second language and uses the parents' native language (Spanish, Creole, Vietnamese, Chinese, etc.) as the language of instruction? This is the approach favored by many professional educators.

Or should all instruction be in English as part of an effort to "Americanize" the child as rapidly as possible? This is the approach vigorously supported by many of the immigrant parents who urgently desire that their children be Americanized as soon as possible. This conflict between professional educators and parents will become a major issue as the new immigration continues.

At this date it appears that the United States is moving toward a bilingual culture (in contrast to the multi-lingual American culture of the late 1840–1920 period) with Spanish being the second language in many parts of the nation, just as French is the second language in Canada. Communities such as Crystal City, Texas, East Los Angeles, California, and Miami, Florida, offer three different models of the bilingual culture which is one product of this new immigration.

Finally, but perhaps most important of all, the new immigration poses a very serious question of public policy. During all of the previous waves of immigration it was widely assumed that the newcomers would melt into American society as rapidly as possible. Frequently this required two or three or four generations, but it was assumed that American society operated on an assimilationist model.

In recent years, however, the "melting pot" theory has been discredited, the 1970s brought a new affirmation of ethnic consciousness, and "pluralism" has become a catchword. Does this mean that many sections of the United States will become bilingual? Or will television, the pressures of upward mobility, suburbia, mass merchandising, bureaucratic pressures, and the educational system swing the pendulum away from pluralism and back toward assimilation?

The assimilation of newcomers is a central question for anyone to raise who is concerned about the impact of the new immigration. The assimilation of "newcomers" also is an important dimension of the urban exodus.

9

The Urban Exodus

After decades of losing population, the 1974 population of Maine was up nearly 1 percent over the 1970 figure.

In the three-year period from 1970 to 1973, 1.2 million more people moved into rural counties in the United States than moved out. This was a sharp reversal of the pattern of the previous quarter century when an average of more than a million people moved out of rural areas each year to go to the city.

Between 1970 and 1974 as many black Americans moved into the South as moved out, a reversal of a pattern going back several decades.

From April 1970 to July 1973 metropolitan counties gained 2.9 percent in population compared to a 4.2 percent increase in nonmetropolitan counties.

In 1966 a Gallup poll reported that 22 percent of the American population stated they preferred city life to living in a rural community. By 1973 that figure had dropped to 13 percent.

Almost all immigrants to the United States from other countries settle in urban counties. Without this influx the population loss of the metropolitan areas would have been twice as large as it was during the first four years of the 1970s.

Rural counties which do not include a town or city with a population of 2,500 or more had a net population loss of 4.5 percent during the 1960s. During the first three and one-half years of the 1970s these counties experienced a population increase of 3 percent.

One representative trend is the migration of retired persons from Chicago to Harrison, Arkansas. West Fork, an Ozark community of 1,247 also in Arkansas, has tripled in population since 1960. One neighborhood on a overlooking West Fork includes fifteen former Chicago families and is known as "Little Chicago."

Cheboygan County, at the northern end of lower Michigan, had a 4 percent increase in population from 1960 to 1970—and a 15.5 percent increase in the first four years of the 1970s.

The large central cities of the nation had a population loss of 1 million from 1970 to 1974.

Much of this migration from urban to rural American has been concentrated in four areas, the Rocky Mountain region, the Ozarks, the Upper Great Lakes, and Southern Appalachia (see map).

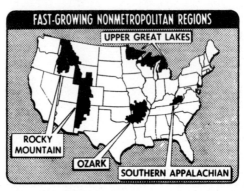

The reasons for this exodus from urban to rural America obviously are at least somewhat speculative, but they include disenchantment with urban life, the migration of jobs to rural counties, the fear of urban crime, a desire to live closer to the soil, the interstate highway system which enables people to live in a rural community and drive back and forth to work, the desire to escape the pollution of urban air and water, the cost of housing in urban communities, the expansion of the tourist industry, and growing nostalgic longing to return to yesterday.

While it is too early to predict the consequences of this migration pattern, it may be helpful to examine a few of the forces behind what some people are calling the New America by looking at one illustration of it.

The New America

Warren County is located in the western part of Kentucky. Its southern boundary is about forty miles north of Nashville, Tennessee. The largest city in Warren County is Bowling Green. It is an outstanding illustration of what is happening in the United States as a result of this urban-to-rural migration. To understand what is happening in Warren County it is necessary to look at four significant population trends in the United States.

The first is the fifty-year decline in the number of farm residents. In 1920, 30 percent of the American people lived on farms. In the early 1970s that proportion leveled off at 4.5 percent. One result has been the decline of thousands of towns which were the trading centers for farming communities. Another has been the decline in the number of residents of several hundred non-metropolitan counties. In western Kentucky, for example, nonmetropolitan counties such as Butler, Logan, and Todd all reached their peak population in 1900 or earlier. Decade after decade, more people move out than move into these and 1,500 other rural counties.

The second trend is the continued increase in the population of more than five hundred other nonmetropolitan counties. Despite the continued population decline in two-thirds of all rural counties, the total nonmetropolitan population has continued to climb from 56.7 million in 1950 to 59.7 million in 1960 to 63.8 million in 1970 to an estimated 69 million in 1975.

The third trend is the decentralization of higher education. In 1950 most institutions with an enrollment of more than 10,000 students were located in metropolitan centers. By 1970 scores of large state universities and colleges had emerged in nonmetropolitan counties.

The fourth trend is highly visible in Warren County—the people go where the jobs go. For decades that meant moving to the city and as a result the metropolitan counties grew by migration from the nonmetropolitan counties. That pattern began to be reversed during the 1960s, however, and between March 1970 and March 1974 approximately 1.5 million more people moved from metropolitan counties than moved in the other direction.

One of the most significant forces behind this last trend has been the United States Department of Agriculture. A major movement to direct future population growth to nonmetropolitan counties was launched during the 1960s when Orville Freeman was Secretary of the Department of Agriculture (perhaps in part because the natural constituency of the Department—farmers—were decreasing in numbers so rapidly?) as part of a national policy to direct a major portion of future population into places such as Warren County, Kentucky. By fiscal year 1972 the appropriations for the rural development programs of the USDA were up to $2.8

billion—double the 1969 figure. A major portion of those funds were designated for housing and for grants and loans for expansion of water supply and sewage disposal system in nonmetropolitan counties.

The results of these and related efforts to reverse the previous population trends can be seen in Warren County. Between 1950 and 1960 the population increased by 6.4 percent, despite the fact that approximately three thousand more people moved out of the county than moved in. This out-migration was offset by the fact that the number of births in the county exceeded the number of deaths for the decade by more than five thousand.

During the 1960s, however, the picture changed. The number of people moving into the county exceeded the number moving out by more than seven thousand for the 1960s. One result of this reversal of the migration flow was that Warren County moved up in the standings when the three thousand counties in the United States are ranked by the number of residents. In 1960 Warren County ranked 670. In 1970 it had moved up to 586 and today is probably about 560.

Between April 1970 and July 1974 the population of the county increased from 57,884 to 61,600 due to (a) 1,900 more people moving into the county than moved out and (b) 4,200 births with only 2,400 deaths for a net natural increase of 1,800. In terms of net migration Warren County is one of the eight fastest growing counties in Kentucky.

Due largely, but not entirely, to the tremendous growth of Western Kentucky University, the proportion of the population age sixty-five and over in the county dropped from 11 percent in 1960 to 9.2 percent in 1970. The proportion of the population *age twenty-five and over* who had completed high school jumped from 32.6 percent in 1960 to 43.4 percent in 1970 and one out of ten adults in the county, *age twenty-five and over,* in 1970 had graduated from college.

Between 1960 and 1970 the city of Bowling Green grew from 7 to 16.2 square miles, from 28,338 to 36.253 residents, and the median age dropped from 27.5 to 23.3 years. In 1970 there were approximately two thousand one-person households among the 10,988 occupied housing units in Bowling Green, and 57.3 percent were owner occupied. One adult out of every seven *age twenty-five and over* was a college graduate, and 6,803 residents were enrolled in college. One out of five employed residents worked in manufacturing, and over half of the employed residents were white-collar workers. One out of ten of the 8,354 families was headed by a woman. The median family income in 1969 was $7,703 ($8,157 for white families and $4,518 for black families), the third lowest among the eight largest cities in Kentucky.

Today Bowling Green and Warren County are outstanding examples of "Tomorrow's America." Tomorrow's America is a term which has emerged to describe those nonmetropolitan counties which have the potential for growth *and the local leaders who are able and willing to turn that potential into reality.*

These are the counties that many national policy makers hope will attract most of the population increase of the last third of this century. During the 1950s it became apparent that while bigger may not be better, bigger is more expensive. The unit or per capita costs of most public services begin to climb very rapidly when a county passes the 100,000 population level. These higher unit costs can be seen most clearly in such public services as police protection, fire protection, traffic control, waste disposal, and environmental controls. In none of these areas of service do the higher unit costs bring a higher quality of results for the residents. In other functions such as education, welfare, and public health many urbanologists are questioning whether the increase in unit costs is matched by an equivalent increase in quality.

These are the nonmetropolitan counties where the population is changing and is beginning to resemble suburban America rather than rural America. When compared to adjacent rural counties the population of Tomorrow's America tends to be younger, better educated, more mobile, less tied to local customs and traditions, more cosmopolitan, expectant of a greater range of choices, more upwardly mobile in terms of vocation and social class, and more willing to take risks.

While it is too early to anticipate all of the consequences and implications of this trend, it is of basic importance to an understanding of tomorrow.

The probable consequences include the continued decline and decay of the large central cities in the Midwest, Northeast, and Upper South; the aging of the metropolitan population and a drop in the median age of the nonmetropolitan population; an increase in the political power of some rural counties which had their influence greatly reduced by reapportionment in the 1960s; an economic advantage in manufacturing in many of these counties since that is where the fruits of recent technological advances are being harvested in new construction; tremendous pressures for rapid changes in the social institutions (see chap. 17) in many of the rapidly growing rural counties; and new stresses on the loyalties of people to the institutions and organizations of society.

83

10
The Changing Sources Of Loyalty

"My great-grandfather, my grandfather, my father, and I had one thing in common—we all went to Yale," commented a forty-four-year-old lawyer. "The other day our oldest son, who will graduate from high school in June, said he wasn't sure he wanted to go to college, but if he did, he wasn't going to Yale!"

"My parents helped start this congregation right after World War I and I've been coming here since I was six weeks old," commented the fifty-six-year-old member of the Maple Avenue Church. "We have three married children. They all live here in this same city, but none of them come to church here. I don't know why, but they don't."

"When my second son decided to go into partnership with me at the store, I thought he also would join the Lion's Club," remarked the sixty-year-old merchant. "It never even occurred to me that he wouldn't, but he hasn't shown the least bit of interest in joining."

"One of the proudest days for my parents," explained the forty-eight-year-old Scoutmaster, "was when I made Eagle Scout. I've been active in Scouting for nearly forty years now, but neither one of our boys shows the least bit of interest in becoming a Scout."

These four comments could be duplicated thousands of times by other parents. They represent a very important trend that is essential in understanding tomorrow. The loyalty of individuals to institutions and organizations is decreasing. Institutions no longer can expect the loyalty of their constituents to be inherited by each new generation. Every organization and institution has to *earn* the loyalty of each new generation.

An outstanding example of this is the American Legion. The Legion, founded in Paris in March 1919, reached its membership peak in 1946 with 3.3 million members. It is now down to approximately 2.7 million members, even though traditionally membership has increased after a war. Relatively few veterans of the Vietnam conflict joined the Legion. The sons of the men who fought in the First World War joined in the late 1940s, but now their sons, who fought in Vietnam, are not joining.

The number of military academies, which have relied heavily on the loyalties of previous generations of students for their new enrollment, have dropped in numbers from approximately 140 in 1949 to less than 50 in 1975.

Perhaps the most conspicuous example of this trend can be seen in the Roman Catholic Church. For centuries loyalty to that church was passed from generation to generation. In 1964, according to the Gallup poll, 71 percent of all Roman Catholics, age eighteen and older, said yes when asked, "Did you, yourself, happen to attend church in the last seven days?" In 1974 this figure had dropped to 55 percent. In 1974 among those age thirty and older, 66 percent of the Roman Catholics said yes to that question compared to 57 percent of those thirty to forty-nine years of age and 41 percent for those in the eighteen to twenty-nine age bracket. (For Protestants the comparable figures for 1974 were age fifty and over 42 percent, thirty to forty-nine years of age 36 percent and under thirty, 30 percent.)

One of the most significant indicators of this trend is

the series of Gallup polls which reveal a growing distrust of American institutions. Less than one-half of the people interviewed expressed "a great deal of confidence" in any of the institutions listed. Organized religion topped the list as 44 percent of the respondents stated they had "a great deal of confidence" in organized religion, while another 22 percent indicated "quite a lot," 21 percent "some," and 11 percent said "very little" or "none."

What Are the Implications?

The implications of this trend not only are of great significance in understanding tomorrow, they also are of basic importance to leaders of the institutions of American society.

First, it is clear that the burden for developing the loyalty of a new generation to any institution rests on the institution, not on the parents.

Second, it appears that loyalty must be earned, it is not automatically inherited.

Third, those institutions which depend on people's loyalty as a heritage from the past are in deep trouble.

Fourth, experience suggests that the loyalty of a new generation is built largely from participation in contemporary goals which (a) are compatible with the value system of the newcomer, (b) provide an opportunity for the newcomer to participate in the formulation of those goals, (c) offer the newcomer an opportunity to express himself, his creativity, and his concerns through participation in the implementation of those goals, (d) provide "satisfactions" for the newcomer when the goal is accomplished or the project is completed, (e) provide an opportunity for the newcomer to become assimilated into the organization through a group, a task, or a role in the goal formulation and implementation process, (f) open the door for the newcomers to be actively involved in shared experiences which are meaningful "community building" types of events, and (g) are relevant to the concerns, value system, and priorities of the newcomers.

In other words, institutions are having difficulty in attracting newcomers and in earning their loyalty by (a) trying to relive yesterday, (b) asking newcomers to help implement goals set by earlier leaders in the organization, and (c) "using" rather than respecting and trusting people.

Fifth, this shift in the sources of loyalty to an institution relates very directly with the change from a survival goal-oriented society to an identity-oriented society (see chap. 3). The issue of people's loyalty to an institution or organization can be understood only in the context of that change. The leader of any institution seeking to win the loyalty of people must do it by involvement, recognition as persons, and participation. It cannot be done by a display of force!

Finally, a key question to raise whenever the issue of loyalty of people to an organization is being discussed can be phrased in terms of the title to the next chapter, "Who is the client?"

11
Who Is The Client?

In July of 1975 the American Federation of Teachers in their annual convention in Honolulu voted unanimously in favor of a massive proposal for early childhood education. This proposal would drop the beginning age to three for children entering public school. Under this proposal, which has widesperad and rapidly expanding support, the 3 million five-year-olds in kindergarten would be joined by another 3 million three-year-olds and 3 million four-year-olds in comprehensive programs of early childhood education which would include social and recreational activities with educational content.

Enactment of this proposal would increase the enrollment of the average school with classes for kindergarten through eighth grade by 15 to 20 percent. Or to put it in comparative terms, this measure would largely offset the decline in elementary school enrollment which has been dropping since the peak year of 1970. Enrollment in kindergarten and grades one through eight in public schools climbed from 19.5 million in 1950 to 27.6 million in 1960 to a peak of 33.3 million in 1970. The steady decline in the number of babies born annually since 1961 means that the enrollment figures for kindergarten through eighth grade will continue to decline until it bottoms out at approximately 28 million in 1985 or 1986. While it would be implemented on a gradual basis, compulsory education for all three-, four-, and five-year-olds would add between 6 and 7 million children to the total enrollment of the nation's schools. Instead of the total elementary school enrollment dropping from a peak of over 33 million to a low of 28 million, the enrollment total would climb to 36 million by 1980 if this plan were adopted and full implemented. Instead of the number of classroom teaching positions being reduced by 160,000 or more between 1970 and 1985, this number would be incerased by at least 200,000 and some estimates range as high as a half million new jobs.

Who is the client for this proposal? Who would benefit from this radical change in the age at which a child first begins to attend public school?

Any attempt to fully comprehend changes that tomorrow will bring must include a response to this question: "Who is the client?"

Who is the client in the above illustration? Who will benefit if this proposal becomes part of the public policy of the nation? The child? The parents? Society as a whole in 1999? The teachers? School administrators?

There is a growing body of evidence that suggests the pre-kindergarten years are exceedingly important in shaping the adult. A substantial portion of the learning processes and the intelligence of the individual apparently are formed during the first five years of life. This does not automatically mean, however, that this can be accomplished most effectively by enrolling three- and four-year-olds in the public schools. There also is an increasing body of evidence which suggests that the expectations placed upon the institutions of society, such as the schools and the churches, far exceed their capabilities (see chap. 5). It may be that the young child will benefit the most by remaining at home with the mother. That was the basic assumption on which the program of Aid to Dependent Children (ADC) was founded forty years ago. It may be that private, profit-motivated businesses could do a better job than the public schools. Others argue that this responsibility for the young child should be given to community groups or to cooperative nursery schools rather than to the public schools. Another group contends that this program for the young child should be combined with day care centers rather than placed in the public schools.

Thus far the focus of the debate on this subject has been on jobs for adults, money, and power. This strongly suggests that the real client for this proposal for early childhood education is not the young child, but is yet to be determined. Among the major contenders are teachers, administrators of the public schools (many of whom overbuilt in the 1960s and this proposal offers a means of filling those empty rooms), proprietors of private nursery schools and operators of day care centers, employed parents of preschool children, officials of the teacher's unions, boards of education, producers of equipment and materials for the nursery school classroom and stockholders in these firms.

In understanding tomorrow it is important to recognize that the identity of the client is changing in many areas of American society. A dramatic illustration of this can be seen in the lawsuits filed against attorneys, auditors, and brokerage firms as a result of the oil-drilling swindle perpetrated by Home-Stake Production Company and the financial shellacking suffering by investors in other bankrupt companies and financial institutions.

In several cases the Securities and Exchange Commission and other federal agencies are contending that the attorneys, accountants, and stockholders involved have a responsibility not only to the firm that is paying them, but also to the individual who buys stock in that company.

This same issue came up in the suit filed by Consumers Union against the Federal Reserve Board. The Board took the position that its clients were the banks which it regulates rather than the public which the FRB presumably represents. The results of the litigation, filed under the Freedom of Information Act, strongly suggest that the regulatory agencies of the federal government must begin to identify the consumer, at least in addition to the businesses they regulate, as a legitimate client.

In early 1974 the *Chicago Tribune* revealed that the Chicago Boy Scout Council had only 52,000 bona fide Scouts, but was reporting an enrollment of 87,000. It quickly became very apparent that one of the clients of the Scouting program was "Boypower 76," a program launched in 1968 to add 2 million boys to the membership rolls of Scouting by 1976. In several inner-city districts, where the costs are subsidized by Model Cities' funds, one-third to one-half of the number of boys on the rolls were not active in Scouting. The combination of meeting a national goal and financing a program drastically altered the identity of the client.

Many people have raised the question about the identity of the real client in regard to the operation of Little League baseball. To many observers it often appears that the real clients are not the youngsters but the parents, coaches, and officials.[1]

This same question can be raised about many Sunday school operations in churches all across the country. The answer often is revealed in such comments as: "We need to put a much greater emphasis on our outreach to children if we're going to fill up all these empty rooms we built back in the 1950s," or "The future of this church rests on the children and youth of today, therefore I favor making the Sunday school the top priority in our planning," or "Mrs. Jones is such a wonderful teacher, it's a shame she only has two or three in her class," or "It seems to me the least the parents could do would be to train the children to be quiet in Sunday school. After all, after preparing for the class the teacher has a right to expect them to listen carefully to the lesson."

This same question often comes up when church leaders talk about the evangelistic outreach of their congregation. Who is the client? Again the answer often can be discovered by listening to comments such as these: "Wherever our minister served before, he always took in at least one hundred new members every year and I know he expects all of us to help him maintain that record," or "The estimate to replace the roof on the church is $28,000, but there's no chance we can do that unless we take in a bunch of new members," or "It seems like every other church in this community is getting a lot of new members except us; I wonder what's wrong with us?"

What Are the Implications?

The most obvious implication of this trend is that here again one can see a means to an end becoming an end in itself and the tendency of institutions to use, rather than to serve, the clientele they were created to help.

This question of the identity of the client is an essential one to raise in any attempt to "renew" an organization and to direct it back to its original reason for being.

An important issue that has emerged in recent years is the demand that the clients be represented on the governing body of the organization providing services to that clientele (see chap. 18). To do this requires a very careful and thoughtful analysis of the question, "Who is the client?"

This question also is central to any analysis of the changing loyalties of people toward institutions and organizations.

This question also is basic to any attempt to define or redefine the purpose of an organization.

Finally, this becomes a very important question to ask when looking at the future of voluntarism in the United States.

12

Voluntarism

In 1971 the California State Superintendent of Schools Wilson Riles initiated a program called Early Childhood Education. Unlike the many "enrichment" programs developed during the 1960s, Early Childhood Education was created to individualize instruction for each child with a heavy emphasis on the early detection and correction of learning problems.

A basic requirement of the program is reducing the pupil-adult ratio from the typical 25 to 1 or 30 to 1 to 10 to 1. This is done by the use of volunteers including parents, grandparents, childless adults, junior and senior high school students, and others. These volunteers help the teachers give each child individual attention. By the end of the 1974–75 school year 280,000 children in kindergarten through third grade were involved in this program in 1,300 elementary schools.

This is but one of many examples which could be offered to illustrate the dependence of our society on volunteers. To a significant degree the direction American society takes in the years ahead will depend substantially on the response of volunteers.

This subject is closely related to and in part overlaps several other chapters in this volume. The changes described in earlier chapters such as the Big Revolution, the shift from survival goals to identity, and shifting emphasis from the functional to the relational are of critical importance to an understanding of the future of voluntarism.

The 700,000 babies who were not born in the 1970s suggests that the twenty-first century may see a critical shortage of young volunteers. The assimilation of the new immigrants from Asian and Hispanic backgrounds will be heavily dependent on the response of volunteers and the formation of new voluntary associations. To a very significant degree the future of those voluntary associations which depend on lay volunteers will vary with the ability of those organizations to win the loyalty of a new generation of volunteers. The organizations which will be most successful in mobilizing volunteers will be those which (a) accept the need to earn the loyalty of volunteers, (b) are able to earn the loyalty of a new generation of volunteers, and (c) affirm that among the clients of that organization are the volunteer staff members and workers.

It appears that the urban exodus will both spark the need for more volunteers and also help develop the context which will increase the supply. This is a point which requires amplification for anyone who is seriously interested in the future of voluntarism and can be illustrated by looking at three different communities.

In western Iowa a community of approximately 5,000 residents includes a small town with a population of less than 3,000 and some 2,000 people on farms surrounding the town. This community is served by more than three hundred voluntary associations including nine 4-H clubs, seven garden clubs, five service clubs, twenty churches, thirteen Parent-Teacher Associations, a group of volunteers at the hospital, a chapter of the American Red Cross, an American Legion post, forty-two different Boy Scout, Girl Scout, and Cub Scout groups, four square dance groups, eight Little League teams, and nearly two hundred other groups, clubs, associations, chapters, and societies.

The response of many active community leaders is that "We're over-organized. We work the same people to death."

A community on the northwest side of Chicago includes approximately 28,000 residents. Recently a list of the voluntary associations in that community was compiled and the list included 425 different organizations including thirty-one churches, thirty-three different Scout groups, four chapters of Alcoholics Anonymous, three chapters of Weight Watchers, seventy-three block clubs and ward organizations, four service clubs, seven lodges, eleven nationality clubs, and 260 other voluntary associations, clubs, societies, teams, and chapters.

In looking at this list one well-known community leader commented, "I guess there are some organizations on that list we could do without, but I would hate to be the one who had to put the finger on them. I don't know whether we are over-organized or whether our problem is that most of the people here won't participate."

In eastern North Carolina, in a rural community of 1,100 residents, someone took a census of all the voluntary organizations in that community, and to no one's surprise, came up with a list of 83 formally organized voluntary associations including seven churches, a fire department, and a community development group.

When he was told of the length of the list a lifelong resident replied, "I thought it would be closer to a thousand! It sometimes seems that we have more organizations than people around here."

In western Iowa there were 300 voluntary associations for 5,000 residents, or an average of 60 per 1,000 population.

In Chicago there were 426 voluntary associations for

28,000 people or an average of 15 per 1,000 population.

In North Carolina there were 83 voluntary associations for 1,100 residents or an average of 75 per 1,000 population.

Why the spread from 15 to 75 per 1,000 residents?

While it would be easy for some readers to move next to a discussion of the "superiority" of the residents of Iowa and North Carolina to the residents of Chicago, that is not the place to find the answer to this question!

Studies of the number of voluntary associations and of the participation of people in them have demonstrated in a very consistent manner that the critical variable is the size of the community. In communities above 10,000 population there usually are five to thirty voluntary associations for every 1,000 residents. In smaller communities the range is between thirty and one hundred per 1,000 residents. As a general rule, the smaller the size of the community, the larger the number of voluntary associations per 1,000 residents and the more widespread the participation of residents in the churches, societies, groups, and organizations of that community. Likewise the smaller the membership of the voluntary organization, the larger the percentage of active involvement by the members. In very simple terms, bigness and urbanization tend to be opponents of voluntarism.

This suggests that the urban exodus may be a key factor in strengthening what some people have identified as the "third force" in American society.

Three other factors which also emphasize the importance of voluntarism in understanding what tomorrow will bring are the increasing complexity of our institutions and society, the rapid rise in the cost of person-centered services, and the responses to scarcity and rising costs.

13
Simplicity Or Sensitivity?

"Sometimes I remember how simple life was in this town and in our church years ago and I kind of long for those days. It seems as though today the churches are involved in everything from civil rights to housing to abortion to amnesty to prison reform. Being a Christian and trying to lead a good Christian life seems to be a lot more complicated today than it was forty years ago," sighed a long-time member of a small county seat town congregation.

If you agree that the comments of this church member reflect the feelings of many people today, it may be helpful to ask *why* the life and ministry of the church is more complex today than it was only a few decades ago, *why* we can expect complexity to increase, costs to rise, and the demand for participatory democracy to increase, and *why* life will be more complex for both individuals and institutions in the 1970s and 1980s than it was in the 1950s.

To some extent that is the question to which this book is addressed. To a limited degree the first half dozen chapters have been addressed to that same question. At this point it may be helpful to state the generalization which is the theme of this chapter on understanding tomorrow.

A comparison of the one-room country school of 1935 and today's larger school system with its array of specialists in speech defects, learning difficulties, and special classes is one illustration of the application of this generalization. This same generalization also can be illustrated by looking at the changes in hospitals during the past quarter century, by reviewing the various proposals to improve the quality of public assistance programs, by contrasting a new automobile with a Model-T Ford, or by looking at the current wave of anti-pollution programs.

In each case the operation has become more complex with the increase in the sensitivity to human need. The same generalization applies to the churches. As the churches become more sensitive to the range and depth of human need they become more complex operations.

This also applies to the formulation of public policy and explains the growing intricacy of the Social Security system and municipal governments. This has led to more responsibility for the life insurance salesperson, the commanding officer of an army post, the principal of a high school, the pastor of a church, the foreman in a steel plant, the president of a labor union, and the head of a corporation in the business of producing energy, to name a few.

This generalization also is helpful in translating certain statements into more meaningful language. An example of this is the nostalgic wish, "I would certainly like to return to the good old days when our church was a simpler operation." When translated this comes out, "I wish we could return to the good old days when we were less sensitive to the needs of other human beings."

A word of caution should be added to the use of this generalization. While a more sensitive response to human need usually increases the level of complexity, an increase in the level of complexity does not necessarily produce an increase in the sensitivity to human need!

The second part of this generalization can be stated in one simple sentence.

The greater the emphasis on human needs, the more costly the response.

This generalization can be illustrated by the rising costs of medical care, public education, highway construction, antipollution controls, public assistance programs, staffing the military services, or providing pastoral leadership in a local church.

In looking at this generalization it should be noted that costs include not only money, but also time, energy, enthusiasm, commitment, dedication, preparation, and skill. A common example of this is the increasing amount of time required of the conscientious church school teacher who tries to be sensitive and responsive to the wide range of needs among the persons in the class. It would be far less costly, in terms of time and energy, to treat each member of the class as though the needs of one were exactly the needs of every other person in the group.

Some of the implications and consequences of this pair of generalizations can be seen more clearly by looking at what is happening to the costs of providing person-centered services.

14
The Costs Of Person-Centered Services

The first car-rental agency was founded in Omaha in the winter of 1915 and after several months of experience the owner charged ten cents a mile, gas and oil extra, with a minimum charge of fifty cents an hour. Sixty years later, when the quality of the automobile has been improved greatly and the purchasing power of the dollar is only one-sixth what it was in 1915, car-rental rates are only slightly higher.

Between 1957 and 1974 the Consumer Price Index rose by 57 percent. During the same period the per student costs of running the public schools increased by 211 percent according to Market Data Retrieval of Westport, Connecticut. In Chicago per-pupil school costs rose 235 percent during that period.

Today it is possible to buy a ballpoint pen for a quarter that is far superior in performance to those costing $7.50 in 1945.

According to the Attorney General of Ohio, physician fees in that state rose by an overall average of 13.5 percent per year in the 1973–75 period.

Leaders in the watch-making industry predict that by 1980 it will be possible to purchase a digital watch for $25 comparable to the ones sold for $200 in 1973 despite a continued wave of inflation.

Several of the larger Protestant denominations are beginning to recognize that by 1980 more than one-half of their congregations will be unable to afford a full-time resident, seminary-trained pastor. In some denominations this figure may be closer to 70 percent. Many of these congregations will be ones which were served by a full-time resident pastor for decades. "Back in the 1930s when times were hard and hardly anyone had any money we had our own preacher," begins the frequently heard complaint. "We're a bigger church now than we were then and everywhere I read about the surplus of ministers, but somehow we can't call one to come and serve our congregation for what we can afford to pay. What's wrong?"

The number of farm-operator families in the United States dropped from 6.2 million in 1940 to 2.5 million in 1975, but the volume of farm production of crops and livestock doubled in that period and the productivity of each farm worker increased nearly fivefold in those thirty-five years. The price of a dozen eggs in the grocery store in 1920 was 70 cents and in 1948 had gone up to 72 cents a dozen. In 1975 eggs cost 79 cents a dozen.

In 1949 a young mother paid seven dollars per day for her half of a two-bed room in the maternity wing of a hospital in Madison, Wisconsin. Today most hospitals charge eight to twelve times that rate.

As recently as 1974 it was possible to purchase a gallon of gasoline at a service station for less than what it cost to buy a gallon of distilled water in the supermarket.

A study of costs for the fall semester at the six state-supported colleges and universities in Kansas revealed that faculty salary costs to enable one student to earn one credit hour for one semester were $16.23 for freshman-sophomore level courses, $31.19 for junior-senior level courses, $58.59 for master's degree courses, and $100.00 for courses at the doctorate level.

The first, third, fifth, seventh, and ninth paragraphs of this introduction represent examples of how technological improvements have enabled the costs of many goods and services to remain relatively constant. The comparatively modest increases in costs in some items have been offset by the improvements in quality and/or the sharp reduction in actual dollar costs in many other items.

The second, fourth, sixth, eighth, and tenth paragraphs illustrate how the costs of person-centered services have skyrocketed in recent years.

What lies ahead is illustrated by the projections prepared by the Oakland Financial Group, a financial consulting firm in Charlottesville, Virginia. They calculated that the costs to the student for a year at a college or university in 1993 will be more than triple the 1975 costs.

This rapid increase in the cost of person-centered services has produced a strong negative reaction in a society which concentrated for decades on the production of goods, in which annual increases in productivity were expected and realized and largely offset increases in wages and salaries. As an ever-increasing proportion of the labor force is employed in providing person-centered services this squeeze in costs will become more oppressive.

How does one achieve an increase in the productivity of a minister preparing a sermon, a lawyer drawing up a will, a surgeon performing an operation, a nurse supplying eight hours of care for a critically ill patient, the teacher of a fifth-grade class, or an author writing a book?

In each case annual increases in wages and salaries exceed any possible increase in productivity.

What Are the Consequences?

What are the consequences of this unprecedented increase in the cost of person-centered services?

One consequence is that it is now more economically viable for Big Ten Universities such as Indiana, Wisconsin, or Iowa to let Ohio State or Michigan win the conference championship in football and go to the Rose Bowl than to go out and recruit (an expensive person-centered enterprise) the football players necessary to win the Big Ten title. When Ohio State or Michigan goes to the Rose Bowl each of the other schools collects one-twelfth of the net gate receipts for the visiting team without the expense of fielding a winning team or making a trip to California.

A second consequence has been to eliminate a large proportion of door-to-door salespersons such as the one who came by a few decades ago to sell vanilla and spices. These small volume sales agents who averaged a relatively small-volume per stop have largely disappeared and been replaced by the Tupperware party, where one stop for the salesperson can produce a comparatively large volume of business, and the Avon ladies, who are mostly part time and do not have to maintain a household from their income.

Many of the far more significant consequences of this trend already have high visibility. These include the increasing scarcity of physicians in many nonmetropolitan counties and the emergence of limited service hospitals, the increasing pressures to improve the productivity of teachers, the sharp decrease in the number of maids and gardeners employed in private homes, the domination of the retail grocery market by supermarkets which enable the customer to fill his or her own grocery list, and the increasing use of para-professionals in many positions formerly filled by more highly trained professionals.

In seeking to understand tomorrow it may be more helpful to divide this subject into two categories, first to single out the rapid rise in person-centered costs as contrasted with the relatively modest increase in the costs of producing food, fiber, and manufactured goods; and second, to identify some of the responses to rising costs. To carry out the second half of that assignment means opening another chapter.

15
The Responses To Rising Costs

It has become increasingly common to hear someone comment that in the early 1970s the United States moved from an era of plenty to an era of scarcity. This is true. Accompanying this statement is the somewhat misleading remark that the era of cheap labor and cheap raw materials is forever behind us. This is excessively simplistic since it overlooks two very basic distinctions.

The first distinction concerns the term "cheap labor." The cost of labor must be measured not only in wages and salaries, but also in productivity. The central point of the previous chapter is that while the increases in productivity have nearly offset the increases in labor costs in the production of foodstuffs, fiber, and most manufactured goods, labor costs required in providing person-centered services have gone up seven to twelve times since 1940 without any significant increase in productivity. That is one reason why the rise in the cost of person-centered services, rather than the increase in the cost of labor, was the central theme of the previous chapter. The other reason for emphasizing the rise in the cost of person-centered services is that every year more people are expressing more concern about the productivity of people working to supply person-centered services. One reason for this is that each year a larger proportion of the labor force is employed in that sector of the economy. The skills at increasing productivity have been developed to the highest level in that sector of the economy—the production of food, fiber, and manufactured products—in which employment is decreasing.

The second distinction concerns cheap raw materials. There is no reason to believe that the era of cheap raw materials is behind us. The most commonly cited example, cheap energy, is the best example. The cheapest source of energy, far cheaper than petroleum, is solar power. Once the technology has been developed to utilize solar energy the people of the world probably will have lower priced energy than ever before in human history. Despite the increase in the price of petroleum, the average consumer works fewer minutes to pay for one kilowatt of electricity or one gallon of gasoline than was true in 1937 or 1947 or 1957. One of the more widely perpetuated fallacies is that cheap and plentiful energy is basic to continued growth. Conservation of energy can mean improvements in the quality, not doing without. In 1974 Denmark, Sweden, and Switzerland all enjoyed a higher gross product per capita than did the United States but used only one-half as much energy to do it.

The critical issue in understanding tomorrow is not that cheap labor or cheap raw materials are in the past, but rather how do the social institutions continue to be increasingly sensitive to the needs of people when the costs of person-centered services are rising so rapidly?

A part of this issue is the impact of rising costs on what economists describe as "labor intensive" occupations and businesses. In many occupations, professions, and businesses, labor accounts for most of the cost of the product or service, and as wages and salaries are increased the cost of the product or service rises accordingly.

That is only one part of this issue, however, and over-looks such factors as productivity, innovation, and creativity. Thus the question arises, how can the organizations providing expensive person-centered services be more open to new ideas on how these services can be provided?

What will be the responses to the rising costs in person-centered services? That, rather than the disappearance of cheap labor or the increase in the costs of certain raw materials is the pressing question in looking at tomorrow.

What Are the Alternatives?

The rising costs of person-centered services will not require huge cutbacks in the quality of services in the years ahead nor a reduction in the quantity of these services, *if* the people responsible want to do something about the problem.

What can be done?

The first step, and the central theme of the previous chapter, is to recognize that a problem does exist.

The next step is to build in a consciousness of costs which often is absent in the organizations which provide person-centered services.

There are many reasons for the lack of this concern over costs. Historically many of these organizations and agencies had a relatively low cost factor because they paid comparatively low wages and salaries. Hospitals, schools, and churches are examples. As the wages and salaries paid by these organizations increased to keep up with the wages and salaries paid people in manufacturing there was no comparable increase in productivity. The higher wages and salaries paid in manufacturing were usually more than offset by an increase in productivity and/or quality. In the hospitals, schools, churches, and other organizations providing person-centered services productivity probably decreased. In 1935 it was not uncommon to find a public school district where the ratio of students to paid employees was 25 or 30 to 1. Now it is more likely to be 8 or 10 or 12 to 1. The same pattern of increasing paid staff while the number of people being served remained the same can be seen in the hospitals, colleges and universities, churches, social agencies, and public agencies.

Another basic reason why many of the organizations providing person-centered services did not develop a consciousness of costs is "the lack of bottom line," there was no easy way to determine whether the organization was making a profit. As long as income offset expenditures everyone was content. If expenses increased, this meant that income had to be raised. It was not until the late 1960s that many of these organizations began to seriously consider the possibility of reducing expenditures rather than increasing income.

Closely related to this was the lack of a "marketplace" for comparisons of costs and quality. It was not until the late 1960s, for example, that private colleges began to feel themselves in a "market squeeze" in competing with publicly supported educational institutions for students. This meant that it was not until the early 1970s that serious efforts were made to measure costs.

Three examples will illustrate what cost consciousness can do in guiding people's thinking. In Boston the cost of maintaining the elevators in public housing projects is $8.12 per month per high rise apartment unit. In Chicago the figure was $7.59 in 1974. When these figures became known, people began to raise questions about the alleged economy of the high-rise apartment projects.

In the late sixties the bookstore at Columbia University was losing money at the rate of $75,000 to $100,000, but everyone knew a university could not function without a bookstore. In 1962 the university leased the operation of the store to Barnes and Nobel. Within a year the university was receiving enough from the lease to cover its costs, and Barnes and Noble were making money. The same story could be told about what happened at Johns Hopkins University when Follett College Book Company leased the bookstore.

A branch bank, which employed three full-time tellers, each on a full five-day week schedule, found the tellers were idle much of the time and customers had to wait in line on Fridays. When they began to look at costs they went to two full-time tellers and one part-time teller who worked only on Fridays.

An operation for removal of tonsils and adenoids in early 1975 cost $169 at Northeast Surgicare in Arlington Heights northwest of Chicago. The same operation at Michael Reese Hospital cost $548 or $381 at the Michael Reese ambulatory surgical facility.

These four examples suggests three different methods of responding to rising costs.

The cost of maintaining the elevators in a public housing project can be paralleled by the "we have to do it a different way" approach followed in an increasing number of organizations. When cost accounting came in, old practices went out the window.

The branch bank example illustrates the possibility of handling the "peak load" problem with part-time help.

The varying costs for the operation to remove tonsils and adenoids reveal the high cost of overhead in a large organization and the temptation in many to level out costs rather than charging full cost for each service.

An example of this can be seen in the many private colleges which charge the same tuition fee for first year students as for seniors, but the actual cost of instruction is two to three times for the senior what it is for the first year student. Just as many large hospitals are losing many potential patients to the ambulatory surgical facilities, the private colleges, by not charging actual costs, are losing many first- and second-year students to community colleges and state universities.

To be more specific, in the future the nonprofit and voluntary organizations providing person-centered services will have to do the following:

(a) Be more conscious of costs.

(b) Use more part-time employees and fewer full-time employees.

(c) Job out many services which it can hire someone else to do for less money than it can provide the service with its own staff.

(d) Charge full cost for each service rendered and let the market place provide more helpful guidance on the range of services offered than is now available when tradition is used as the guide.

(e) Be very conscious of peak hour costs and vary charges accordingly.

(f) Depend more heavily on para-professionals and volunteers.

(g) Be open to new methods of providing traditional services.

(h) Eliminate the non-productive segments of the operation.

(i) Be willing to recognize the real choice is not between the status quo and change, but rather is between adaptation and disappearing from the scene.

Now, how can these concepts be applied?

For illustrative purposes let us turn to the 110-member Oak Grove Church. For at least forty-five years the membership of this rural Kansas open-country congregation has fluctuated between 90 and 130. Oak Grove Church had its own full-time resident minister until 1945. When the parsonage burned on Palm Sunday in 1945, the minister who was sixty-nine, decide to retire and the congregation made a "temporary" arrangement to share a preacher with the church in town of the same denomination. This arrangement continued until the fall of 1975 when the church in town served notice they planned to terminate the arrangement in June 1976. That congregation has grown to the point where it wants its minister there all Sunday morning.

What can the Oak Grove Church do?

Let us review the above list.

(a) They are already very conscious of costs.

(b) They can choose and seek a part-time minister.

(c) They might "job out" the preaching by finding supply preachers for Sunday morning.

(d) They might double their giving level and go out and call a full-time minister.

(e) They might recognize the peak hour problem and ask the church in town if they could share the services of that minister by holding worship on Sunday afternoon.

(f) They might seek para-professionals and volunteers to assist supply preachers.

(g) They might be open to the new idea of becoming part of a larger parish and sharing staff with several other congregations.

(h-i) They might decide that if they cannot continue as they have for the past several decades, they will dissolve the congregation rather than change.

If the Oak Grove Church can seriously consider all but one of the alternatives on that list of ways of cutting costs it should be relatively easy for any other organization to do the same!

Regardless of the techniques and procedures used to control costs, there is one built-in cost that is really an obligation contracted by yesterday's generation to be paid off by tomorrow's generation. The magnitude of it means that it must be considered by anyone seeking to understand what tomorrow will bring.

16
The Pension Problem

In the summer of 1975 a bus driver with an annual salary of $13,000 retired at age fifty with a lifetime pension of $15,600 annually. How did he do it? He worked an average of thirty-five hours a week overtime for his last year, and this boosted his total salary to over $30,000. Under the state law governing the pension plans for New York City policemen, fire fighters, and transit employees, he was entitled to retire any time after he had twenty years of service and had passed his fiftieth birthday. At retirement his pension would be one-half of his earnings for his final year. For his 1,824 hours of overtime in that last year this bus driver not only collected over $17,000 in overtime pay, he also added $750 a month to his pension check for every month for the rest of his life!

In Detroit and Los Angeles a city policeman or fire fighter receives fifty cents of pension benefits for every dollar of salary he earns. The city of Philadelphia had unfunded pension liabilities of over $900 million at the end of 1972, far more than its entire bonded indebtedness and nearly double the unfunded liability back in 1968. At the end of 1973 the unfunded pension liability for the city of Pittsburgh was $225 million, for the city of Allentown $27.5 million, and for The United Methodist Church $461 million.

The 200 largest corporations in the nation have unfunded pension liabilities of over $30 billion.

An unfunded pension liability means the years of service have been performed to earn pension credits, but the money has not been set aside to cover this pension claim, a claim which will not come due until the employee retires. Whenever the pension payments for prior years of service of an employee are increased, this unfunded liability increases. At Uniroyal, for example, the company agreed in 1960 to pay each employee on retirement a monthly pension equal to $2.25 times the number of years employed at Uniroyal. This created an unfunded prior service claim of $147 million. By 1973 the agreements with the unions had boosted this to $9.50 a month, times the years of service, and the unfunded liability had jumped to $531 million.

General Motors Corporation has $6 billion in these unfunded prior service pension claims. Chrysler has $1.8 billion in unfunded pension liabilities—an amount equal to two-thirds of the value of all the Chrysler common stock outstanding.

The state of Illinois has a $1.6 billion unfunded liability in the state teachers' retirement and is not expected to have a full funded system before 2023—when most of today's teachers born before 1940 will be dead.

In 1974 the editors of *Fortune* interviewed the senior financial officers of 545 large corporations and found that payments into pension programs and profit sharing plans in 1973 were equal to one-fifth of the after-tax profits of these companies. At Ford Motor Company pension costs were equal to 9 percent of pre-tax profits in 1964 and over 50 percent of pre-tax profits ten years later.

By the end of 1976 private pension funds will have

115

accumulations of assets (which are considerably less than the liabilities) of $200 billion.

The unfunded pension liabilities for ministers in all of the annual conferences in The United Methodist Church at the end of 1974 was equal to more than twice the salaries paid all pastors for that year. Since in the end the pension claim for United Methodist ministers is really a claim on the congregations, the unfunded liability on each congregation averaged out to more than twice what they paid in ministerial salaries in that year.

What Are the Consequences?

What does all of this have to do with understanding the future? What is the relationship between pensions and the future? Without going into exhaustive detail it may be helpful to lift up only four implications of the pension problem which will be influential in the years ahead.

1. The pension agreements entered into by the large cities and many of the larger suburbs practically guarantee a continuation of the urban exodus described in chapter 9. The clerk who retires at age fifty-five with twenty-five years of service in Philadelphia can expect an annual pension of $7,685 plus Social Security benefits. In Houston the figure is $6,683. A school teacher who retires at age sixty after thirty years of service can expect, on the average, a total of $158,121 in pension benefits in Philadelphia, while a Philadelphia policeman who retires at age fifty after twenty-five years of service can expect to receive $282,188 in pension benefits.

As the years go by and pension agreements already entered into become payable, these cities have no choice but to reduce services or raise taxes. In New York City the pension payout will be at least $3 billion annually by 1985.

In many cities and private corporations the assumptions on which the pension projections are based are obsolete or irrelevant. People are living longer, and therefore the payout period will be longer on individual pension payments. Many pension funds have been operating on the assumption of 7 percent annual return on their investments, but in the 1968–75 era several averaged a minus 5 percent return! If a cure is found for cancer and new and effective treatments are discovered for heart problems, many pension funds will be in severe difficulty. The only good news in recent years from the medical front for managers of pension funds is that each year an increasing number of women are dying from lung cancer.

2. The baby boom of the 1946–1960 era has produced an increasing number of newcomers into the labor force who want jobs and promotions. In the past a normal part of the response to this pressure has been to lower the age when people leave the labor force to retire. In one of the larger Protestant denominations, for example, there is an active proposal to encourage pastors to resign from the larger churches when they reach their sixtieth birthday and to retire denomination executives at age sixty. It was suggested that the pension board lower the retirement age from sixty-five to sixty to encourage this. Their response was very simple, "Who will pay it?"

In the fall of 1972 The United Methodist Church in the United States had forty-five bishops on active duty and forty-two retired bishops. Would the churches favor reducing the age of retirement in order to increase the number of job openings for younger ministers?

Basically the question is, Will the people born after 1945 be willing to pay more money into pension funds, to the Social Security Administration, and through payroll taxes in order to open up more jobs and more promotions for younger people?

3. As the years roll by the impact of the missing 700,000 (see chap. 7), the babies who weren't born in the late 1960s and the 1970s, will be felt. If they had been born, they would be at work in the year 2020 to help pay the pension benefits of the babies who were born back in the 1950s. Will the fifty-year-olds of 2020 be willing to carry this increasing load? Or will they vote to cut Social Security payments? Will they move to disfranchise anyone over age sixty-five who is not an active member of the labor force? The generation gap may become real when the 3.2 million babies born in 1973 are asked to pay for the pensions of the 4.1 million babies born in 1955.

4. One unexpected result of the Employee Retirement Income Security Act (ERISA) of 1975 is that smaller companies are abandoning their pension plans at the rate of four thousand annually. This means an increasing number of persons in the labor force are not covered by a private pension program.

5. The increasing importance of pensions as a part of the employee's total compensation package means a decrease in vocational mobility. Leaving one's job can be very costly when a comparison is made of pension benefits or when the employee can become fully vested by remaining with the same employer for two or three additional years. This pattern already is clearly visible among employees of local governments and Protestant ministers.

6. Proposed mergers of large organizations can be stymied by the unfunded liabilities of the organizations' pension funds. Thus a merger of the United Church of Christ and The United Methodist Church would be difficult because of the huge unfunded pension liability of the United Methodists. Would Detroit want to annex Hamtranck and assume responsibility for an unfunded liability of $24 million in the Hamtranck police and fire pension fund?

7. For the past several years the private pension (exclusive of Social Security and state and municipal pension funds) and employee benefit systems have been growing at a rate of 14 percent compounded annually. This mean a doubling in size every five and one-half years. Thus the $175 billion in assets in these funds would reach $350 billion by 1980, $700 billion by 1985, and $1,400 billion in 1990. That last figure is twice the January 1975 value of all stocks listed on the New York Stock Exchange. It already is clear that pension funds are the major prop under the stock market and that the decisions of a few pension managers can cause the market value of any one stock to fluctuate sharply. By 1985 or 1990 will the fluctuations of the stockmarket be controlled by the pension funds rather than the whole economy? Where will all of this money be invested? Will the managers of the pension funds emerge as the new power structure of American society? What will be done to regulate their behavior? To a significant degree the pension system is a part of a much larger pattern which is producing a significant redistribution of wealth in the United States and—among other consequences—producing a rapidly growing group of comparatively wealthy widows.

17
The Redistribution Of Wealth

During World War II, when wages and salaries were regulated, the idea emerged of increasing an employee's compensation through payments into a pension fund. Private pension funds, which had been only a minor item in the compensation of employees in 1935, began to flourish. In 1935 only 2.7 million workers were covered by private pension plans. This number jumped to 6.4 million by the end of World War II, and the idea was firmly planted in the employee compensation program of the nation. Today more than 35 million workers are covered by private pension plans which have reserves of over 200 billion dollars—nearly 100 times the reserves of 1940.

Social Security coverage has been greatly extended, and the benefits have been increased many times and are now tied to a cost-of-living index.

During the past twenty years the number of married women living with their husbands and employed outside the home has increased from 8 million in 1950 to 20 million in 1975, and slightly over one-half of these have children under eighteen years of age. (There are another 8 million single women in the labor force, plus 5 million more who are either widowed or divorced).

Today approximately 33 million families own their own single-family home, and 40 percent of these do not have a mortgage. By contrast in 1910, 1920, 1930, and 1940 less than one-half of the homes in the United

States were occupied by the owner. Most families rented. Today nearly two-thirds of all housing units are occupied by the owner.

In 1950 the average family was covered by life insurance policies with a total face value of $4,600. Today the average family has $25,000 of coverage in life insurance.

Those five paragraphs are one part of a two-part package which is producing a redistribution of wealth unparalleled in human history. This nation is in the process of making obsolete the biblical reference to poor widows. It is now common for a husband to retire from his job with a home paid for, $20,000 to $50,000 in life insurance, a private pension, generous Social Security benefits, several thousand dollars in savings, and a wife who also may be ready to draw benefits.

The second part of this package is reflected in the changes in the life expectancy tables. In 1920 the life expectancy of the forty-year-old white male averaged thirty years compared to thirty-one years for the forty-year-old white female. In 1971, thanks to the obviously discriminatory practices of medical science, the life expectancy of the average forty-year-old white male was thirty-two years compared to thirty-eight years for the forty-year-old white female.

As a result this husband dies a few years after he retires. He leaves a widow who is typically two or three years younger and therefore still has a life expectacy of eight to ten years. Increasingly her real income is nearly as large as it was when her husband was working, and she no longer has a husband to feed, clothe, and house out of that income! The result is an increasingly large number of widowed women who are financially more secure than when she and her husband were both employed in order to send three children through college and one through graduate school.

This trend is built into the economy and will become increasingly visible in the 1980s and 1990s, when more and more widows are able to benefit from two pensions plus Social Security plus substantial life insurance benefits.

Perhaps the most significant redistribution of wealth within the nation is concealed by some overly simplified reporting on income distribution. In February 1974 the Council of Economic Advisers reported that the one-fifth of the population with the lowest income received only 5.1 percent of total personal income in 1947, and by 1972 this had gone up only to 5.4 percent for the lowest fifth. By contrast, one-fifth of the population received 43.3 percent of the total personal income in 1947, and by 1972 this had dropped only slightly to 41.4 percent received by that top one-fifth. The top 5 percent of the population received 17.5 percent of all personal income in 1947 and 15.9 percent in 1972.

These figures suggest only a slight redistribution of income over the period of a quarter century.

There are three factors which should be taken into account when reading these numbers. When these are considered it appears that a very significant redistribution of income tax has taken place since the end of World War II.

First, one-fourth of all households have an annual income under $5,000 a year, but many do not have anyone in the labor force. In 10 percent of these households the head is under twenty-five years of age, and in 46 percent the head of the household is over sixty-five years of age. It also should be noted that 78 percent of these low-income households are either one-person or two-person households.[1]

Second, the proportion of the population sixty-five and over has increased from slightly over 6 percent in 1947 to over 9 percent in 1972. Since older persons tend to live in smaller households, and live in part off accumulated wealth (a mortgage-free house, for example), this also distorts the distribution figures.

Third, the number of one-person households has increased from 4.7 million in 1950 to 12.6 million in 1973 —an increase of 168 percent. During the nine-year period the number of two-person households increased from 12.5 million to 20.6 million, but the number of households composed of three or more increased by only 33 percent from 26.3 million in 1950 to 35.1 million in 1973.

What has happened is that the increasing affluence of the United States has enabled many people—the elderly, the student, and the single adult—to live by themselves, and this has distorted the income distribution figures.

According to Simon Kuznets and others who have studied this subject in detail, if one counts only those households headed by a male age twenty-five to sixty-four there has been a very marked increase in the equality of incomes during the past quarter century.

On the national scene there have been many forces at work which have fostered a redistribution of income and wealth. In addition to the Social Security and the pension systems mentioned earlier, this list would include Medicare, the recent increases in the price of coal and the resulting impact on Appalachia, the various state programs to equalize school taxes, unemployment insurance, food stamps, and public assistance.

The biggest factor by far in this picture is the federal

government. The technical term "transfer payments" is used to describe that portion of the federal budget that is part of a deliberate effort to transfer income from one group to another. In 1945 only three cents of each dollar of personal income came from these transfer payments (Social Security, veterans' benefits, unemployment compensation, public assistance, Medicare, and food stamps). By 1965 that proportion was up to seven cents out of each dollar of personal income, and by 1975 it had doubled again to fourteen cents. The dollar total channeled through these transfer payments totaled $150 billion in 1975, five times the 1965 total.

One of the most subtle forces for accomplishing the redistribution of income has been the combination of the federal income tax and inflation. Inflation has pushed many families into a higher tax bracket, even though their "real" income did not rise. As a result, in 1974 when personal income increased by 8 percent, less than enough to keep up with a 12 percent increase in prices, there was an increase of 15 percent in federal income taxes.

On a smaller scale, the government of New York City has been involved in a systematic effort to redistribute income through a tuition-free city university, rent controls, and an extensive welfare system. To a lesser degree the same pattern can be seen in nearly every state and in many other large cities.

On the international scene the big factor in the redistribution of income has been a result of the huge increases in the price of petroleum. Thus nations such as Iraq, Kuwait, Libya, Iran, Saudi Arabia, Norway, and Venezuela are among the "newly rich" nations of the world. A reasonable guess is that, while petroleum prices probably will drop sharply by the early 1980s (in terms of constant dollars), the action of the OPEC nations mean a new era has been launched in the redistribution of income and wealth on a global scale.

What Are the Implications?

It may be helpful to lift up four implications of this trend which have not received much attention thus far.

1. The redistribution of income in the United States has been a major factor, perhaps the biggest single factor in the housing shortage and of the boom in apartment construction. The net increase in the past quarter century of 8 million one-person households and over 8 million two-person households, as contrasted to the increase of only 7 million households with three or more persons, has been the factor on the demand side which has supported the housing market.

2. Today many long-established congregations are caught among the pressures of maintaining large, old physical plants; rapidly rising costs; a plateau in the level of giving by members; the temptation of members to depend on the endowment fund rather than to increase their own level of giving; the preferences of many people to give to designated causes such as missions, outreach, property improvements, or youth ministries; and the growing number of older people who are living off a combination of current income and accumulated capital and who are concerned lest they outlive their money and have to be dependent on others. Understandably some of these people may feel severely limited in current giving, but they do want to give to their church. The church can help them in this dilemma by encouraging them to include the church in their will. Perhaps the best approach to this is to incorporate as a separate legal entity a trust or a

foundation to which people may give out of current income, to which they may give memorials, and which can be designated as the beneficiary for bequests. Scores of churches have followed this procedure which can assure the donor that the stipulations will be followed, which removes temptation from the governing board of the congregation to "borrow" from endowment funds, and which also makes financial assistance available to the congregation for both internal and outreach ministries. In general, congregationally controlled endowment funds tend to have a blighting impact on stewardship while foundations tend to have a creative and helpful impact. In many congregations the trustees are members who hold that one position of responsibility for that period of time. This restriction strengthens the arms-length relationship between the congregation and the foundation and reduces the temptation for the congregation to become heavily dependent on the foundation. It also opens the door to use of the matching-grant concept.

3. The combination of financial independence, better health, and work experience means that one of the most important sources of volunteers in our society is this growing number of economically secure widows. The number of widowed women in the population has increased from 3.9 million in 1920 to 8.3 million in 1960 to over 10 million in 1974. Today one out of every seven women eighteen years of age and older is widowed. This group includes some of the most creative people in our society, and together they constitute a tremendous pool of talent. (By contrast the number of widowed men has dropped from 2.3 million in 1950 to 2.1 million in 1970 to 1.9 million in 1974. Only one out of thirty-five men eighteen years of age or older is widowed.)

4. This redistribution of wealth, which to a substantial degree has been for the benefit of the elderly, is almost certain to result in some form of backlash by the turn of the century or shortly thereafter. A decreasing proportion of younger people in the labor force will be paying, directly and indirectly, for the benefits received by older persons. By the year 2020, if not sooner, this could produce a major political crisis pitting the productive working people in the labor force against a very large number of voters in the older age brackets.

Thus far a crisis has been avoided by "baking a bigger pie" each year so that no one's piece is reduced in size even though the share received by others grows larger. *If* the nation switches to an intentional "no growth" policy, a position advocated by many, this will hasten the arrival of this political crisis.

5. The redistribution of wealth is the major issue of of dividing the United States, Japan, and Western Europe from the Third World. The United States and other technologically advanced nations have contended that the best method of increasing the income level of people in the Third World is by baking a larger pie. This emphasis on increasing production does not appeal to many of the leaders from the Third World. They want to shift the debate from increasing the size of the pie to the size of the slices. This "New International Economic Order" would mean that the rich nations would pay more for what they purchase, reduce the prices of their exports, and reduce their standard of living by 20 to 40 percent.

(For a fascinating and very disturbing novel on this theme, read *The Camp of the Saints* by Jean Raspail [New York: Scribner's, 1975].)

18
The End Of The Search For Simple Answers

The Growing Demand for Participation

There are four separate, but related generalizations which will be used to close this volume. Each one stands alone as an important factor for the person seeking to look into the future, but each one is in part a product of the trends described in the earlier chapters. Each generalization should help the reader understand the changing reality of the world around us and some of the frustrations produced by those changes.

One of the products of the trends described in previous chapters is both extremely important to grasp and very difficult to implement. One result has been that it has more slogans than results.

The first of these is becoming increasingly visible with the passing of each day.

The more complex the program, the greater the demand for participation by those who will be affected by the program or organization.

In part this is a product of the Big Revolution. As institutions are organized to accommodate people it naturally follows that many of the people will want a voice in the changes that are being made to accommodate them.

In part this is a product of the reversal of the flow in the civilizing process described in chapter 2. As the people born in the early post–World War II years began to see during the 1960s that they were influencing the value systems of older adults, it naturally followed that this would be accompanied, among other changes, by a demand to lower the voting age.

In part this generalization reflects Glasser's definition of a change from a survival goal to an identity society and the accompanying change in the basic method of motivating people from power to involvement, participation, and cooperation.

In part this is a reflection of the changes described in chapter 4—from the primary emphasis on the functional to a growing emphasis on the relational dimensions of life.

Likewise, as loyalty of people to the institutions of society moves from inherited to earned this sparks a demand for participation by those whose lives will be affected by that institution.

Perhaps the most important of the sources of this development is identified in chapter 13. The more sensitive an organization is to the needs of people, the more complex its operation—and the more likely that that organization or institution will be sensitive to and encourage the demand for participation by the clientele.

This generalization also is a partial explanation for the contemporary demand for participatory democracy. Examples of this demand can be seen in schools where the students are demanding a voice in the policy-making, in the federal programs to control agricultural production which call for a referendum among the farmers, in urban renewal and model cities programs, in churches where many members are calling for a decentralization of the decision-making process, in the variety of anti-poverty programs, in the administration of public assistance programs, in the decision-making process in the typical American family, in the debate over legalized abortion, in the struggle over the governance of prisons, in the policy-making processes of hospitals, in the operation of public housing projects, and in both the women's liberation and the juvenile rights movements.

Where is the Resistance to Change?

One of the most disappointing discoveries by people in the human potential movement also is very important for anyone seeking to understand tomorrow.

The organization or institution developed around the interaction of persons tends to be more resistant to change than organizations developed around the production of goods.

"I can't understand why this congregation is so strongly opposed to any changes in our church," commented a young pastor three years out of school. "Most of the members are either farmers or retired farmers, and I marvel at how easily they have adapted to the many changes that have occurred in agriculture during the past thirty years. But when it comes to any change in how we do things in the church, they insist on doing it the same way their grandparents did it."

This generalization may help this young pastor understand why his congregation can accept change more readily in their farming methods than they are willing to accept changes in their church. This generalization also helps explain why there was relatively little resistance to the construction of the interstate highway system which brought communities closer together, but there was great resistance to the consolidation of rural schools which also brought communities together. This generalization also helps explain why there has been little resistance to the changes in the employment patterns which see an increasing number of adults driving thirty to sixty miles each way to work every day, but there is great resistance to using the school bus to reduce racial segregation in the public schools. This is also evidenced in strong national sentiment in favor of most forms of interdenominational cooperation, but a resistance to any proposal to merge congregations across denominational lines.

While any explanation of the "why" behind the trends and generalizations described in this volume obviously include a large measure of speculation, this may be one of the easiest to explain. First, man is a social creature and relationships with other people are more important than relationships with "things." Second, as Glasser has pointed out, an ancient human need has been for man to be with fellow men. Third, everyone needs a reliable and predictable reference point. As the "things" of this world change, the relationships with people become that reference point. Fourth, people tend to be more threatened by other people than by objects or things; therefore the changes which may alter the relationships of people with one another are more threatening and therefore are resisted more vigorously.

While it is a logical corollary to the earlier generalization which is the theme of this chapter, the part of this concept which disturbs many people in the human potential movement is that *the better the quality of the interpersonal relationships among the members of a group, organization, or institution, the more resistant that organization is to change.*

A translation of that into plain everyday English is

that organizations developed around the interaction of people naturally are resistant to change and the better the quality of those interpersonal relationships, the more opposition there will be to changing the status quo.

Does that help explain some things you have been wondering about at home or at the office?

The Problem-Solving Illusion

Most hotels have light bulbs in hard-to-reach locations. In New York City, where electricians on a hotel staff receive $7.50 an hour, it may cost $5, $10, or even $15 to replace one of these high, hard-to-reach bulbs.

One approach is to replace the standard bulbs, which burn for 750 to 1,000 hours, with the special long-burning bulbs that last 3,000 hours.

Does that solve the problem?

No. It simply means trading one problem for a different problem. The hotel has reduced the cost of replacing burned-out light bulbs, but the light produced by the longer lasting bulbs is less adequate and produces eye fatigue. Instead of solving the issue, the hotel has traded off its problem and created one for the persons using that hotel.

A parallel situation can be seen in the efforts of the manufacturers of the 1970–74 model automobiles to reduce air pollution. The pollutants coming from the exhaust of the automobile were reduced, but the trade off was a reduction in gasoline mileage. Abandoning the automobile for the horse or vice versa is merely trading one form of pollution for another. In general each change in energy sources decreases dirt and pollution, but each change creates other trade offs.

It now turns out that the acidity of the rain falling

on the eastern United States and on Europe has been increased to as much as one thousand times because of the air cleaning devices on factory smokestacks. Because these devices remove the particles of solid matter, which formerly neutralized gases such as nitrogen oxide and sulfur dioxide, the rain now is much more acid.

Rarely are problems solved. Far more often one problem is traded off for another problem—and hopefully it is a trade up rather than down.

When a church happily bids farewell to a minister and eagerly awaits the replacement many parishioners feel their problem has been solved. It has not been solved. They merely have traded one set of problems for a new and different set. This concept of trading one set of problems for a different set is of basic importance for anyone looking at the future.

For centuries much of the effort to predict the future has been heavily flavored with the hope that the passage of time will produce solutions to contemporary problems. Examples include the expectation that the young child will "outgrow" a speech defect or an allergy, the prediction of the young husband that "by next August our income should begin to exceed our expenditures and we'll be able to save some money," the belief of the leaders of the local chamber of commerce that "new industry will solve our problems," the dream of the parents that "as soon as our youngest is through school we'll be able to relax," and the quadrennial promise that if the voters "will elect our candidate as the next President of the United States our problems will be solved."

Each attempt to solve a problem brings to mind again that statement of Garrett Hardin's, "You can never do merely one thing."

That is why it may be helpful to end this book with a brief review of what came to be known as Forrester's Law.

Forrester's Law

Rarely has anyone packed more wisdom into a seven-word sentence than California biologist Garrett Hardin when he wrote, "You can never do merely one thing." Sometimes referred to as Hardin's Law, this sentence could serve as the introduction to the last chapter of this book.

The 1960s produced at least two important streams of thought that continue to influence the thinking of many people as they look toward tomorrow. One is the optimism that was behind the social activism of the Kennedy-Johnson era and operated on the assumption that if only good people would try harder, most of the injustices and inequities of American society could be erased. Out of this came the movement for a Great Society.

Caught up in this stream were politicians, church leaders, social workers, businessmen, teachers and foundation executives as well as leaders of minority groups.

The second stream began a little later and has won many converts from the other stream. It now includes many people who are taking a more realistic view of the complexity of the problems of American society and are shying away from simplistic answers to complex problems. A representative voice is that of Harvard professor James Q. Wilson who said, "I have not heard an intellectually respectable defense of criminal rehabilitation." [1]

The research which has been done on social problems and their cure has produced many shockers for those who were convinced that every problem had a simple solution.

One of these was the year-long study in Kansas City which revealed that increasing or decreasing the amount of police patrol in an area did not significantly affect the crime rate nor did it affect the attitudes of people about the danger of crime. For literally centuries conventional wisdom has insisted that increasing the visibility of the police in an area will reduce crime—but apparently it makes no difference.

For decades architects and city planners operated on the assumption that by building vertically rather than horizontally it would be possible to provide both high density residential development and large open spaces for parks. The Pruitt-Igoe development in St. Louis and scores of other public housing projects have torpedoed that piece of conventional wisdom.

A very widespread bit of conventional wisdom is that elevators are unreliable and often dangerous in the event of fire in a high-rise building. A two-and-a-half-year study, partly financed by the National Science Foundation, conducted by researcher Vladimir Bazjanac found that the use of the modern elevator usually is the fastest and safest method for evacuating people from a high-rise structure.

For more than twenty years and the use of $40 million worth of advetrising Smokey the Bear helped broadcast the message that forest fires are bad—until in the early 1970s foresters finally concluded that the health of the forest requires occasional fires. The new policy in the Grand Teton National Park, for example, is to let fires which are caused naturally burn until they burn themselves out.

In looking at these and many other complex issues we

now have the benefit of what has come to be known as Forrester's Law.

The more complex the situation, the more likely the intuitive response will be counterproductive.

This generalization is often referred to as Forrester's Law in recognition of the contributions of Jay W. Forrester who declared, after detailed research of efforts to solve contemporary social problems, that in complex social systems "intuitively sensible policies can affect adversely the very problems they are designed to alleviate." [2]

Examples of this law can be found in the construction of high-rise public housing apartments to ease the problems of the urban poor, construction of off-street parking garages to reduce traffic congestion, aid to families with dependent children, slum clearance projects, and the many different programs to subsidize the farmer.

Among the many other examples that could be used to illustrate Forrster's Law are the following: Mobile x-ray screening units may be doing more harm than good. The federal subsidy for construction of sanitary sewers under the clean waters legislation has encouraged unsound and expensive community expansion. More energy and scarce resources are required to clean the returnable soft drink bottles than are used in making a new one. Increasing the amount of time a student spends in school does not increase what the student learns and may teach bad study habits. The demand that the FHA insure homes in the inner city so more whites would remain in the central city was finally implemented in the early 1970s with the result that a flood of white families who previously had been unable to find a buyer sold and fled to the suburbs. The Volstead Act of 1919 which was supposed to eliminate drinking and enforce moral virtue turned out to be a means of creating a large organized crime network. The Brooke Amendment to the public housing legislation which set a limit of 25 percent of income that a federally subsidized public housing project could charge a tenant is causing many projects to become slums because now there is no money for maintenance or repairs. The indeterminate sentence designed to let an offender out of jail when the authorities believe he has been rehabilitated and is ready for release has produced an irresistable temptation for prison authorities to use this as a means of manipulating prisoners and has generated bitterness rather than rehabilitation. The new federal campaign law apparently means that candidates will be using their campaign contributions largely for raising money rather than for campaigning.

These are only a few of the many examples that could be cited to illustrate Forrester's Law. Problem solving is not as simple as it once appeared to be. In fact, it may be worth asking, is it possible to "solve" problems?

Notes

Introduction

1. John and Evelyn Dewey, *Schools of To-morrow* (New York: E. P. Dutton, 1915), p. 246.
2. John Kenneth Galbraith, *The Affluent Society* (Boston: Houghton Mifflin, 1958).
3. For a critical analysis of the expectations of computers see Fred Hapgood, "Computers Aren't So Smart, After All," *The Atlantic,* August, 1974, pp. 37-45.
4. For a more extended discussion of the energy shortage of the sixteenth century and its consequences see Andrew Hardy, "Man's Age-Old Struggle for Power," *Natural History,* October, 1973, pp. 82-86.
5. For a more detailed examination of the nature and benefits of the scenario approach see Herman Kahn and Anthony J. Wiener, *The Year 2000* (New York: The Macmillan Company, 1967), pp. 262-64.
6. Lyle E. Schaller, *The Impact of the Future* (Nashville: Abingdon Press, 1969).
7. The Club of Rome is a group limited to one hundred members, drawn largely from industrial leaders and establishment intellectuals who share a very pessimistic view of the future, perhaps because the group includes so very few Third World members. A useful analysis of their perspective is offered by B. Bruce-Briggs, "Against the Neo-Malthusians," *Commentary,* July, 1974, pp. 25-29.
8. Elisabeth Kübler-Ross, *On Death and Dying* (New York: The Macmillan Company, 1969).

Chapter One

1. For a more extended discussion of nominating procedures see Lyle E. Schaller, and Charles A. Tidwell, *Creative Church Administration* (Nashville: Abingdon, 1975), pp. 29-38.
2. Quotes in "Catholic Women to Become Priests?" in the *Chicago Tribune,* July 26, 1975, Section 1B, p. 9.
3. For a more extended discussion of this concept see Lyle E. Schaller and Charles Tidwell, *Creative Church Administration* (Nashville: Abingdon, 1975), pp. 38-44.

Chapter Two

1. Margaret Mead, "The Oldest Postwar People," *The New York Times,* January 21, 1973.
2. *Ibid.*

Chapter Three

1. William Glasser, *The Identity Society* (New York: Harper & Row, 1972).

Chapter Five

1. Andrew M. Greeley and Peter H. Rossi, *The Education of Catholic Americans* (Chicago: Aldine, 1966).

Chapter Eight

1. Quoted in Oscar N. Olson, *The Augustana Lutheran Church in America* (Rock Island, Ill.: The Augustana Book Concern, 1950), p. 40.

Chapter Eleven

1. For a critical evaluation of the Little League program by one of the great baseball pitchers of recent years see Robin Roberts, "Strike Out Little League," *Newsweek,* July 21, 1975, p. 11.

Chapter Seventeen

1. Irving Kristol, "Taxes, Poverty, and Equality," *The Public Interest,* Fall, 1974, pp. 6-7.

Chapter Eighteen

1. Quoted in *Newsweek,* June 30, 1975, p. 22.
2. Jay F. Forrester, *Urban Dynamics* (Cambridge: The M. I. T. Press, 1969), p. 70.

Bibliography

Bell, Daniel. *The Coming of Post-Industrial Society: A Venture in Social Forecasting.* New York: Basic Books, 1973.
  Among the more lasting significant contributions of this widely quoted book are the author's identification of the clash between equality and meritocracy, the key role of bureaucracy, and the emergence of a scientific elite and a positive attitude toward social forecasting.

Berry, Adrian. *The Next Ten Thousand Years: A Vision of Man's Future in the Universe.* New York: Saturday Review Press, 1974.
  This volume along with Maddox's *The Doomsday Syndrome,* provide two of the more optimistic views of what the future may bring. Both are written by Englishmen, both are based on solid studies of current scientific research, and both affirm technology as an ally, rather than identify it as an enemy. This exceptionally well-written volume is as readable as most science fiction.

Bettmann, Otto L. *The Good Old Days—They Were Terrible!* New York: Random House, 1974.
  This veteran archivist has assembled here a selection of graphic photographs which speak for themselves. These pictures, accompanied by a sparse text, reveal that life was a difficult, and often dreary, struggle for survival in the four decades following the end of the Civil War.

Brosseau, Ray, and Andrist, Ralph K. *Looking Forward.* New York: American Heritage Press, 1970.
  At the turn of the century, several magazines printed articles on what life would be like during the 1900s. This large book is a collection of articles, editorials, and cartoons with a heavy sprinkling of advertisements that reflect the

optimism of the 1895–1905 era. The predictions range from one that suggested the coming abundance of electrical appliances would make women happy to stay in the kitchen forever, to one that argued China would not be able to become an important political power during this century, to another which predicted that stairways in private homes would be replaced by automatic elevators.

Chaplin, George, and Paige, Glenn D., eds. *Hawaii 2000.* Honolulu: The University of Hawaii Press, 1973.
This is the report of a conference called by the governor of Hawaii in 1970 to define the questions and problems that will face that state during the last decades of this century. Among the most important sections of this provocative book are the ones that describe the efforts to develop a future orientation among the citizens and the description of the alternative futures.

Commoner, Barry. *The Closing Circle.* New York: Alfred A. Knopf, 1971.
This pessimistic small volume has become a classic in the battle against ecological disaster. This should be read along with Maddox's counterclaims.

Ehrlich, Paul R., and Ehrlich, Anne H. *Population, Resources, Environment: Issues in Human Ecology.* New York: W. H. Freeman, 1972.
This, along with Dr. Ehrlich's earlier volume *The Population Bomb* and the famous Club of Rome Report, are the contemporary versions of the Reverend Thomas Malthus' famous argument of 1797 that continued population growth inevitably brings disaster.

Falk, Richard A. *A Study of Future Worlds.* New York: The Free Press, 1975.
This is an exceptionally thorough and extensive study of world order, of radical changes in the distribution of resources, and of a greatly expanded international organization that can facilitate peaceful change.

"Footnotes to the Future" is a four-page newsletter published twelve times a year by Futuremics, Inc., 2850 Connecticut Avenue N. W., Washington, D.C. 20008.

Futures: The Journal of Forecasting and Planning is published by IPC Science and Technology Press Ltd. IPC House, 32 High Street, Guilford, Surrey, England GU1 3EW. It is published six times a year and is primarily concerned with emerging techniques and methods in forecasting.

The Futurist was first published in 1967 and is the official publication of the World Future Society: An Association for the Study of Alternative Futures, P.O. Box 30369, Bethesda Branch, Washington, D.C. 20014 and appears six times yearly.

Greeley, Andrew M. *Religion in the Year 2000*. New York: Sheed and Ward, 1969.
Father Greeley, one of the most prolific writers of our era, criticizes the current arguments that science has replaced religion and argues that a hundred years hence religion and God will still be alive and well.

Heilbroner, Robert. *An Inquiry into the Human Prospect*. New York: W. W. Norton, 1974.
This is one of the more notable of a series of very pessimistic books that came out in the early 1970s. Heilbroner sees the United States at the end of an era with a planned state capitalism the next stage.

Kahn, Herman, and Bruce-Briggs, B. *Things to Come*. New York: The Macmillan Company, 1972.
One of the best known futurists and a historian combine to produce the sequel to *The Year 2000* with the focus on the 1970s and the 1980s rather than on the year 2000. Some readers will be unhappy with the "value free" approach, and others will see it as an anti-elitist volume.

Kahn, Herman, and Wiener, Anthony J. *The Year 2000*. New York: The Macmillan Company, 1967.

This remains one of the pioneering classics on suggesting a disciplined and systematic approach for the study of the future. The more useful contributions include the concept of "surprise free" projections and the use of scenarios for describing the future.

Maddox, John. *The Doomsday Syndrome*. New York: Mc-Graw-Hill Book Company, 1972.
This is a systematic rebuttal of the pessimism of the prophets of gloom and doom by a British scientist who contends that science and technology are not enemies, but rather are essential to the survival of the human race.

Mesarovic, Mihajlo, and Pestel, Edward. *Mankind at the Turning Point*. New York: Dutton/Readers Digest Press, 1975.
This is a successor study to the very pessimistic first Club of Rome Report, *The Limits of Growth,* and uses a greatly improved computer model which, among other improvements, recognizes regional differences, and emphasizes that delay in facing worldwide issues will be very costly and may produce major regional catastrophies.

Moore, Richard E. *Myth America 2001*. Philadelphia: The Westminster Press, 1972.
In this hopeful book a United Presbyterian executive contends that men use myths to conceptualize their experiences and there is identifiable sequence to the emergence of these myths. Moore discusses the current collision of three of these myths—Christianity, Scientism, and the Counterculture.

Muller, Herbert J. *Uses of the Future.* **Bloomington:** University of Indiana Press, 1974.
In this outspoken, critical, and at times pessimistic book, one of the "grand old liberals" describes his speculations about the United States in the year 2000 and offers both a diagnosis of the present state of affairs (such as the declining value placed on creativity and a moral code) and a prescription for making this a more humane nation by the end of this century.

Population and the American Future. United States Government Printing Office, 1972.

This is the final report of the Commission on Population Growth and the American Future appointed by President Richard M. Nixon in 1969.

Prehoda, Robert W. *Designing the Future.* Philadelphia: Chilton Book Company, 1967.

One of the pioneers in linking technological forecasting with long-range planning has written an excellent introduction to forecasting the future. Its major defect is that it was written before the "scarcity syndrome" of the early 1970s altered people's perspective about the future.

Rapid Population Growth—Consequences and Policy Implications. Baltimore: Johns Hopkins, 1971.

Schaller, Lyle E. *Impact of the Future.* Nashville: Abingdon Press, 1969.

The author identifies twenty basic trends and analyzes their impact on society in general and the church in particular.

Shuman, James B., and Rosenau, David. *The Kondratieff Wave: The Future of America until 1984 and Beyond.* New York: Dell Books, 1974.

The authors use Nikolai D. Kondratieff's economic theory to project the future of America for the bright 1970s and the dark days of the 1980s. They emphasize the parallels of the 1970s with the 1920s and the 1980s with the 1930s.

Technological Forecasting and Social Change is published by the American Elsevies Publishing Company, 52 Vanderbilt Avenue, New York, N.Y. 10017.

This technical journal was first published in 1969 and today is the outstanding American technical quarterly in the field of futurism.